SOMERSET CIDER

The Complete Story

Philippa Legg & Hilary Binding

Somerset Books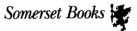

First published in Great Britain 1986 as *So Merry Let Us Be*
This second revised edition Copyright © Philippa Legg 1986, Hilary Binding 1998

British Library Cataloguing in Publication Data
A CIP record for this title is available from the British Library

ISBN 0 86183 460 7

SOMERSET BOOKS
Official Publishers to Somerset County Council
Halsgrove House
Lower Moor Way
Tiverton EX16 6SS
Tel: 01884 243242
Fax: 01884 243325
www.halsgrove.com

The financial support of Somerset County Council
for this publication is gratefully acknowledged

Printed and bound in Great Britain by
Bookcraft (Bath) Ltd, Midsomer Norton

SOMERSET CIDER

THE COMPLETE STORY

Contents

A rare and unspoilt hillside orchard in Somerset. James Ravilious

Chapter 1
An Historical Introduction

We've come up from Somerset, where the cider apples grow,
We've come to see your Majesty and how the world do go;
And if you're wanting anyone will you kindly let us know,
For we'll come up from Somerset because we love you so!
                                                Somerset Folk Song

Somerset and cider are, like fish and chips, inextricably linked, and have been for centuries although the origins of cidermaking in the county, as in the rest of Britain, are lost in the mists of time. Apples are indigenous to this country; oral history tells of one apple variety at least being introduced by the Romans who also planted orchards, however. It is likely that a cider rather like a Rhenish wine was being made with apples from the great monastic orchards at places like Canterbury and Ely before the coming of the Normans. Cider apples may have been introduced into Somerset from Brittany and the Normans would almost certainly have encouraged cidermaking as a way of producing alcohol in colder areas on the fringes of grape-producing country. At the end of the twelfth century, William of Malmesbury recorded that Glastonbury was also known as Avalon, 'Apple Island', a name that was largely romantic invention and may have had little to do with apples. Nevertheless the countryside around Glastonbury is still renowned as one of the best cider apple growing areas in the county.

A medieval toper at Muchelney Abbey.   James Ravilious

Much of Somerset was suitable for growing apple trees and the first written references to cider appear in ecclesiastical accounts. In 1230, Jocelin, Bishop of Bath, received a grant which referred to cider presses and later, in 1242-3, cider and apples appear as sources of profit to the bishopric. As a valuable commodity, bequests of cider figure in Somerset wills; in 1557, for example, William Garland of Dinnington left a legacy of one hogshead while inventories drawn up for probate often list quantities of cider, ready for drinking. When William Higgins, carpenter of Baltonsborough, died in around 1738 his goods included ten hogsheads of raw cider and one more, as well as five hogsheads of cider which had been 'boiled with hops', doubtless to improve a rather thin pressing.

Between 1650 and 1750 cider grew in popularity (or at least figured more frequently in documents). At this time an increased interest in natural science, encouraged by the foundation of the Royal Society in 1660, and the difficulty in obtaining French wines because of the continental wars, revived the appreciation of cider, particularly by members of the upper classes. 'The Credit of Cyder being of few late years much advanced in the Estimation of our best Gentry', wrote Dr Beale of Yeovil in 1656.

In 1664 John Evelyn recorded a wager between a vintner and a country gentleman, the latter claiming that he could produce a cider which would excel the vintner's best Spanish or French wines. A majority of the judges found in favour of cider. Defoe wrote in 1726: 'So very good, so fine so cheap ... great quantities of this cider are sent to London, even by lane carriage tho' so remote, which is evidence of the goodness of it beyond contradiction.'

In 1678 John Worlidge published *Vinetum Britannicum*, a comprehensive book on the growing, grafting and care of cider apple trees. He detailed the processes of cidermaking and included diagrams for the construction of cider machinery. Worlidge maintained that if his suggestions were followed 'cider in a little time would wear out the reputation of French wines and by degrees lessen the expence of Malt.'

Title page and illustrations from Vinetum Britannicum, *John Worlidge (1678)*

The cider boom of the late seventeenth and early eighteenth centuries declined as European trade improved and people began to drink more grain-distilled liquor and other spirits. The imposition of a tax on cider in 1763 was a further blow to the industry. The tax, requiring the maker to pay four shillings per hogshead of cider, was very unpopular. For the first time a government officer was given the right of entry to private premises to search for dutiable goods. William Pitt the Elder popularised the phrase 'every man's house is his castle' in fighting this law. In Somerset feelings ran so high that Charles Kemeys Tynte MP was compelled to

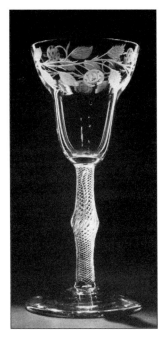

A large perry glass (left), decorated with apples and pears.
A cider glass (right), both c. 1752. Newton Freeman

a toast to the friends of Liberty, the night was spent
with a joy peculiar on so happy an occasion.
Reprinted in the *Western Gazette*, 1966

In the late eighteenth and early nineteenth centuries interest in cidermaking revived. The need for improved self-sufficiency during wartime had boosted the making of cider in the 1650s and did so again during the Napoleonic Wars (1789–1815). At these times cider was advocated with near-patriotic fervour. In 1656 Dr Beale proclaimed, 'If we must be hindered of Trade with Spain, I wish our English Indignation would scorn to feed at their Tables, to drink their liquors, or otherwise to borrow or buy of them or any other of their confederates, as long as our Native soil did supply us with Necessaries' while in 1810, J.W. Parsons wrote, 'I have the greater pleasure in giving away the grafts and the genuine recipe for making cider in the hope that it may add to the number of those who "love the land they live in" and think with me that English liquors are best suited to English constitutions.'

publish a declaration stating his opposition to the tax. In 1766 the tax on home-produced cider was repealed and there was great rejoicing. At Milborne Port in Somerset, the festivities were considerable:

Thomas Medlycott Esq., one of the Members, had two hogsheads of cyder brought from his seat at Ven to the town Cross (music playing and bells ringing), with a young apple tree in a barrel, the apples and leaves gilt with gold and silver, and a young man striding a barrel carried a gilt staff and frame bearing the inscription 'By Providence of God and a British Parliament, Liberty was restored, July 5th. 1766'. After drinking

Techniques of orchard care and cidermaking were recorded in nationwide surveys commissioned by the Board of Agriculture in the 1790s. John Billingsley, in *A General View of the Agriculture of the County of Somerset* (1797), recommended the quality of Taunton Vale cider: 'It is supposed they possess an art peculiar to themselves, of conducting the fermentation and thereby preserving a rich and delicious flavour.' William Marshall in his *Rural Economy of the West of England* (1796) barely referred to cider in the Somerset section, having dealt with the topic in Devonshire. He disapproved of the use of good land being used for orchards and thought too much effort and interest were devoted to the subject.

Enthusiasm for agriculture and horticulture at that time produced various scientific works. T.A. Knight wrote *A treatise on the culture of the apple and pear* in 1801, and an illustrated *Pomona Herefordiensis* in 1811 while The Bath and West of England Society, founded in 1777, began to publish its 'Letters and Papers' in 1780 to encourage good agricultural practices. Various articles on cider appeared, and the Society offered a prize of twenty guineas in about 1808 'to the person who... shall make... three hogsheads of cider, from as many different sorts of apples, keeping all the sorts perfectly unmixed; all such sorts of Cider to be superior in strength, richness and flavour, to any Cider generally made in any part of this kingdom.' Later in the 1870s J. Scott, an expert orchardist of Merriott in Somerset, published an informative catalogue of varieties.

By the mid-nineteenth century the reputation of cider had fallen. It survived mainly as the refreshment of farm labourers and a component of their wages and was made for local consumption on most Somerset farms. However some ciders from Herefordshire and, notably, cider from Heathfield Rectory at Taunton travelled to markets in many parts of England. The general view was 'that ciders and perries are all alike and only to be distinguished from vinegar by a highly discriminating palate'. (Radcliffe Cooke).

A few people realised that good money might be made from selling cider to the growing urban population. In Herefordshire, the Woolhope Club and Radcliffe Cooke MP, known as the Member for Cider, supported and investigated cider production. The Woolhope Club commissioned the splendid illustrated *Herefordshire Pomona* which was published between 1876 and 1885. The Hereford firm of Bulmers was expanding and beginning to experiment with

Pioneer of cider research and the cider revival, Robert Neville Grenville, 1846-1936. Squire of Butleigh from 1886.

champagne-type ciders. In Somerset, research was centred on Butleigh Court where, from 1894, the squire, Robert Neville Grenville, and the chemist, F.J. Lloyd, were carrying out similar experiments. This research was funded by the Board of Agriculture and The Royal Bath and West of England Society and continued for ten years.

The Butleigh cider team c 1895.

Neville Grenville's attempts to make a stable cider for bottling were hampered by the lack of scientific work on yeasts and fermentation. He knew that well-financed research was proceeding abroad and, with other members of the National Association of Cidermakers, made moves to establish a proper research station in Britain. As a result of their efforts, the National Fruit and Cider Institute was founded at Long Ashton in 1903. It aimed to promote the scientific study of cider-making, in an attempt to raise the level of uniformity and profitability of the beverage. For the first time a comprehensive classification of cider apples was attempted. Apple trees were sent out from the centre and these formed the basis of experimental orchards in Herefordshire and the West Country. Highly successful annual cider-tastings

were introduced from 1906 in order to promote the work of the Institute amongst local farmers and gentry.

During the early years the Institute was perpetually short of money. However in 1909 its fortunes improved when it was chosen as the national research centre for fruit and cider, and granted money from the Government's Development Fund. This caused much wrath amongst Kent's fruit producers, who hoped their own county would gain this honour, and they resorted to establishing their own privately-funded station. The future of the Institute was assured when it was formally linked to Bristol University in 1912, with whom it has provided valuable information to the cider industry ever since.

Neville Grenville was astute in his forecast for the cider industry:

It undoubtedly will be the lot of comparatively few farmers to become first rate cidermakers ... His premises are often utterly unsuited for it, and his mind is not trained to work with the accuracy or science such a highly chemical process needs. As homemade beer and small breweries have died a natural death in favour of large breweries under highly trained experts and a business staff for the sale of their product, so will cidermaking for the British public have to be conducted by people who make it their special study.

He thought it the role of the farmer to provide quality cider apples to larger cidermakers. His prediction was fulfilled in the 1920s and '30s when many small businesses burgeoned, selling to local pubs and clubs. Most of these had disappeared by the mid-1950s and only those with modern efficient machinery and scientific production methods, like Coates of Nailsea, Bulmers of Hereford, Taunton Cider, Gaymers of Norfolk, and a handful of others, survived to dominate the cider market. Although the farmer had lost his hold on the commercial market, particularly as breweries started to tie their pubs to their own cider production in the 1930s, he continued to make cider for himself, his workers and friends.

An interest in quality was kept alive by the agricultural shows and the national prizes awarded by the brewers and allied trades. At the turn of the century there was great rivalry to produce the best cider. When in 1902 a Somerset cider was champion, Farwell reported in the *Bath and West Journal* that the Devon men thought it too sweet and only fit for women and children.

During the 1940s and '50s the large cider businesses struggled, while some of the farmhouse cidermakers lost interest. Apple orchards were allowed to decay and many disappeared, a situation not helped by the availability of government grants for grubbing up orchards. By the early 1960s the demand for cider was increasing and the large companies launched big publicity campaigns and introduced policies for the maintenance of good orchards. As cidermaking became more profitable even on a small scale, a tax on cider and perry was reintroduced. Although unpopular with the small cidermaker the tax has not deterred the general public in their enthusiasm for cider which continues to support cider production in a variety of forms from the small farmer to the large company.

Gold medal for cider presented in 1932 to S.J. Sheppy.

At present there is, as well, a revival of interest in apple orchards and old apple varieties, fuelled by growing concerns for conservation in the landscape and preservation of local heritage, while the growth of the tourist industry in Somerset provides another incentive for keeping the tradition of farmhouse cidermaking going.

Chapter 2
Apples and Orchards

An' there vor me the apple tree
Do lean down low in Linden Lea.
William Barnes, 1801-1886

Small orchards of old trees can be found in many places in Somerset, nestling in the valleys of the Brendon Hills and grouped round farmhouses on the Levels. The trees thrive in the rolling sandstone country of the Devon and Dorset borders and in small stone-walled enclosures in the Mendip villages.

Maps and memories record a landscape full of orchards but now, in most parts of the county, few remain. Recently, an elderly lady climbed up to Butleigh monument expecting to see the Spring apple blossoms, only to find that the wonderful sight she had known from childhood had disappeared. A map of Carhampton dated 1827 shows the centre of the village full of orchards. Today, one of the few that remain has been saved by villagers from being built over and has become a community orchard.

Several factors have led to this decline in the number of orchards. Cider is no longer needed to sustain the farm workforce while the use of heavy machinery on farms has made the drinking of cider during work unwise. Fewer visitors call to be offered refreshment and modern farming developments have encouraged the growth of other crops with government grants available in the 1960s for grubbing up orchards. In 1894 there were 24,000 acres of cider orchards in Somerset; in 1973 there were just 2,499 acres. In the past fifty years at least 60% of Somerset's traditional orchards have disappeared though this decline has now been checked.

Although the number of orchards has diminished, yields have increased considerably with improved care and techniques and the introduction of bush trees. In general, a well tended bush orchard can yield 8 to 15 tons to the acre against 4 to 10 tons for a standard orchard. Bush trees also start to crop earlier, at about five to seven years old, while a standard tree will be cropping fully at fifteen to twenty years. Standard trees are still most common in Somerset, often growing 30 to 40 feet high with a long trunk and broad canopy.

Although all cidermakers will defend their local product, some areas are especially renowned for growing good cider fruit, and these include the localities of Wedmore, Glastonbury and Baltonsborough, Martock and Taunton. This is probably due to a variety of factors, such as soil type and quality, suitability of apple varieties, micro-climate and husbandry. Even in a good area, orchards right next to one another will be valued differently by an experienced cidermaker. One thing most of these places have in common is calcareous and gley soils with alkaline to neutral acidity.

Traditional orchard on the Somerset Levels. James Ravilious

They tend to be grey-brown in colour, and are clay over impervious calcareous clays and shales, and therefore imperfectly drained. John Worlidge, an experienced orchardist writing in 1678, recommended the following soil. 'For Cyder-Fruit chuse a good warm light Rye-land: for the heavier, colder and moister Wheat-land is not so good, the Cider being not so Clear nor Vinous.'

He thought the soil could not be too light since the more the fruit 'inclines to redness, the better'. He also thought that an orchard planted 'on dry or rising ground' would bear fruit that 'will yield a more Vinous liquor'. Dr Beale of Yeovil, writing in 1656, also preferred apples from soil 'less deep' since the apple that comes from richer and lower ground 'is more pallid, more plump, but more waterish and

14

Modern Somerset orchard with standard trees. James Ravilious

insipid'. The apples grown on the sandy soils at Merriott and Seavington St Mary have a good reputation. It is true that a hot summer and dry soil will produce apples high in sugar content from which cider strong in alcohol can be made. Worlidge also noted that 'if your land decline a little to the South East, it is esteemed the best Situation of Land to plant Fruit trees on.' This is still thought good practice because such an orchard is protected from the east winds in the spring which check bud growth. The trees gain the benefit of the morning sun and are protected in the autumn from the south-west winds. They are also less liable to frost damage.

Good orchard maintenance involved the liming of trees. On a damp morning the lime was put in heaps

15

around the orchard to slack. 'Then when it was slacked we used to lime the trees by throwing the lime over them.' (John Brown). This killed lichen and reduced the habitat for insects. Tree trunks were also painted with a mixture of whitewash and cow-dung to deter cattle. Occasionally the trunks were ringed with brambles or old barrel staves for protection.

One of the great skills of apple growing is the use of grafts to propagate the desired varieties. It provides the trees with the strength and other qualities of the stock. In the past the stock was the vigorous crab-apple. Worlidge gave detailed instructions. If the stock was between one and three inches one should 'cleave it, that the slit may be on the smoothest side of the stock, and fit your Graft, shouldering it at a Joint or Bud, joyning the insides of the Rinds exactly.' If the stock exceeded three inches the graft was best made into the rind or bark, a passage being made for the graft with a wedge. This he commended since 'thus you may set many grafts round the stock.' Stock under one inch could be whip grafted, the two slanting sur-faces joined and bound with 'Hemp, Yarn or Basse'. To protect the graft from rain and other damage it was covered with 'Lute or Clay mixed with new Horsedung', which in Somerset was called 'Cat' and was used until recently. If the stock was small, hot wax was used instead and grafters heated it in a small cauldron in the orchard and then moved very quickly to coat the graft before it set.

A good grafter possessed a natural ability for the job or 'green fingers' and was highly valued. It was said of a famous grafter in North Wootton that if he graft-ed his pipe, it would grow. He had to be knowledge-able about the right times to graft, the local soil variations and the suitability of varieties for different

Grafting. James Ravilious

locations. Grafters were known to make mistakes and one family in the West Pennard area was notorious for confusing their grafts and producing trees of unex-pected varieties – perhaps too much cider was drunk while the work was going on!

In Somerset it has been the practice to plant standard trees so that cattle or sheep can graze beneath the branches for nine months of the year. When the apple harvest begins, the stock are removed and sometimes the grass is cut. An old saying in the north of the county, that one must 'Hain-up come Priddy Fair Day' (i.e. the third week in August), refers to this practice. This supports the view held by several older cider-makers that the seasons are running later, since now harvesting does not generally begin until mid-September.

Although most apples can be used for cidermaking, in Somerset it has been the tradition to use cider fruit, that is, varieties more closely related to the wild crab-apple. Their bitter astringency derives from the tan-nins and acids they contain, although the type and amount vary considerably with variety, soil and cli-mate. Apple varieties have been divided into four main categories: sharps, bittersharps, bittersweets and sweets:

	Acid	Tannin
Sweet	below 0.45%	below 0.2%
Bittersweet	below 0.45%	above 0.2%
Bittersharp	above 0.45%	above 0.2%
Sharp	above 0.45%	below 0.2%

Sharps include cooking apples while sweets include table fruit. The Hereford Broadleaf is so high in tannin that its apples have been used for tanning leather. The variety Tom Putt was often planted in cottage gardens, because it could be used for eating, cooking and cider and it became known as 'the cottager's apple'.

In the past, cider was made from bittersharps but modern taste prefers sweeter ciders and now the mix often contains about 75% bittersweets with some sharps which help to provide the necessary acidity to stop the cider turning black.

A single cider apple variety may have many names while different localities have distinct varieties limit-ed, perhaps, to a few orchards. This has prevented the compilation of a definitive *Pomona* for Somerset, although a beautifully illustrated example was drawn for Herefordshire in 1811. One historic apple is the Somerset Redstreak. Over the years it may be that many different apples were given this name but in 1670 Dr Beale recorded one. 'This apple is here called Meriot-Ysnot, and great store of them are at Meriot, a Village not far distant: Possibly this Meriot may prove to be the Red-Strake of Somersetshire.' The Meriot-Ysnot was very similar to the Hereford Redstreak, as is the modern Somerset Redstreak; it is a mild bitter-sharp, good for blending with other fruit and adding sparkle to the cider.

Trees were often grown from seed. These 'wildings' sometimes produced fine apples, the variety then being maintained by grafting. Two Somerset exam-ples are Yarlington Mill and Dunkerton Late Sweet. Mr Bartlett, who was born at Yarlington Mill in 1898, remembered the first apple tree of that name:

...it was grown from a pip, or gribble (the Somerset word for a young sapling grown from a pip) that grew out of the wall by the water wheel. My Grandfather planted it in the garden to graft when big enough but after a year or two it bore fruit, a nice bittersweet apple, and it made good cider so it was never grafted and they called it Yarlington Mill.

The Dunkerton Late Sweet was another wilding that quickly began to bear fruit in the 1940s. The original tree which was discovered by Bill Dunkerton, a local grower, is now in its prime in an orchard at Baltonsborough and has become a recognised cider apple variety.

As new trees are developed there is a tendency for the old varieties to die out or stand forgotten in old orchards. The old Kingston Black is always recalled by cidermakers, but there are few trees left. It is an unusual apple combining all the qualities necessary to make good cider; a mild bittersharp which gives a sparkle to the drink. However, it has poor yields, is liable to disease and doesn't like dry weather, so is rapidly being replaced by more robust varieties. One variety that appears to have died out completely is the Cockagee, an Irish import that was first cultivated around Minehead in the mid-eighteenth century. It was often praised, the cider being 'full-flavoured, soft, creamy yet vigorous, it was preferred to any champagne'. The last known reference to it was on a bottle label found in 1920.

During the last few years there has been a sharp revival of interest in old apple varieties. Somerset varieties have been researched and recorded by June Small of Charlton Orchards, near Taunton, and her *Guide to the Origins of Somerset's Apples* lists 158 varieties that are thought to originate from Somerset. (See page 73.) Many enthusiastic owners of orchards are now planting traditional varieties rather than newer, more commonplace trees.

Apple trees tend to bear biennially and this characteristic can become more marked when dry summers are followed by cold springs. The situation can be partially remedied by regular pruning, the use of chemical sprays to inhibit bud growth or by manual de-budding. In a good year harvests can be early and the first apple used for cider is the Morgan Sweet – these are gathered when green and hard but are not considered true cider apples. They make a light cider which ferments quickly but does not keep well and was always intended to be used before Christmas. It fills a gap when there is little of the previous year's cider left and it is still made in some places for the harvest supper. In the early twentieth century Morgans were packed in round willow baskets and sent to Wales where, according to one apple grower, the miners used to eat them with Caerphilly cheese for lunch.

Sometimes apples were 'poled' from the trees, and occasionally large sheets were spread out round a tree which was then shaken and the apples caught in the sheet. Far more often the apples were left to fall naturally although these days machinery is used to shake the apples off the trees in bush orchards. The fruit was generally picked up by women and children who were quicker at the work although some men made a living at it – particularly if they were small and didn't have to stoop too far. It was unpleasant work picking rotting apples from the frozen grass in November and December and the willow baskets would get grassy, wet and heavy. Earlier in the autumn wasps were often a problem.

The apples were first collected into a 'picker' holding a peck or about 20 pounds, although some women would put them in their aprons and then tip them into a three-peck basket holding 50 to 60 pounds. These tall, two-handled wicker baskets had many names: wooley butt, quarter sack basket or maund. In the 1920s and '30s pickers were paid 6d for picking one or

Harvesting apples at Trull, 1934.

two of the larger baskets. Since a mature standard tree in a good year can produce 5 to 7 hundredweight, or about 28 to 35 basketfuls, it can be seen that a lot of hard work was needed to make a cider cheese holding a ton of apples. In the Exmoor region where withies are not grown, apple baskets were oval, without handles, and made from ash staves; these were also known as maunds.

In the past, and occasionally today, apples were left in long heaps in the orchard to ripen or 'come'. One early eighteenth-century writer, John Newbury, insisted that apples should 'lye together in a hoard, at least till the usual time of their Maturity, that the Cider otherwise is seldom or never worth the drinking.' John Worlidge said that a mature apple could be gauged by its colour, rich fragrant odour and the blackness of its kernels,

19

Picking up apples. James Ravilious

immature fruit 'hath not onely been the occasion of much thin, raw, phlegmatick, sowre, and unwholesome Cider but hath cast a reflection on the good report that Cider well made most rightly deserves.'

Worlidge thought the heaps of apples should not be left outside but placed on dry straw, out of the sun and rain. Certainly many Somerset cider cellars have an apple loft above them where apples could be left until they

20

Picking up apples.   James Ravilious

were ready. The apples were then gently rolled across the floor to separate them from twigs and leaves and 'stirred down' through a hole to the apple mill placed below. Neville Grenville, always inventive, developed a dry-cleaning device consisting of a wooden trough, tilted from the apple loft to the mill, on the bottom of which bevelled batons were nailed to slow the speed of the apples. The debris, unable to roll over the batons, remained stranded and the slow-moving apples could be picked over by hand.

Much of the folklore relating to apple trees has been forgotten in the twentieth century but some still think that the sun must shine through the trees on Christmas Day for a good harvest, or that the trees should be well-covered with snow in the winter to be fruitful. An old and probably accurate adage was noted in Scott's *Orchardist* of 1873:

> *If Apples blow in March, for Apples you may search;*
> *If Apples blow in April, Apples will be plentiful;*
> *But if Apples blow in May, you may eat Apples Night and Day.*

Apples give a curious impression of 'disappearing' after they have set because the leaves cover them. This has given rise to maxims such as 'Apples disappear with the mowing scythe and come back with the reap-hook' and 'Apples disappear at sheep shearing and come back with the harvest.'

An apple basket used for transporting apples by train.

Chapter 3

Cider as a Way of Life

A drop or two of cider will do us no harm!
                    Somerset Wassail Song

THE TRADITION OF FARMHOUSE CIDERMAKING

The practice of farmhouse cidermaking has declined considerably during the twentieth century; these days there may be just one working press remaining in a village where previously there were half a dozen or more. Nevertheless, the cidermakers that are left, and many other country people, feel that there ought to be cider on farms in Somerset and that apple trees should be part of the landscape. This old affinity, rooted in an earlier agriculture, survives or dies depending on the social networks within the rural community. In the past one element of this was the type and size of landholding.

Although Somerset was a large county and had notable landowners like the Luttrells, Earl Poulett and the Bishop of Winchester, their estates were let out in small units on short leases to tenant farmers. John Billingsley, writing in 1798, felt there were few things that operated a more powerful check on improving agricultural practice than short leases since 'where a man's tenure is precarious, and subject to the whim and caprice of a landlord, little improvement can be expected.'

Some writers on agriculture thought that far too much interest and energy was expended on ciders. 'Their Orchards might well be styled their Temples, and Apple Trees their Idols of Worship,' wrote William Marshall in 1796. 'I wish to see them (orchards) confined to unculturable sites, and to have them considered, as they really are, a subordinate object of husbandry.'

But this was an uncongenial idea and agreements between landlord and tenant often required the maintenance of orchards which were considered by most to be essential to the running of a farm.

Orchards are kept up by arrangement between the landlord and tenant. In the east the landlord finds trees and the tenant plants them, in the west, the tenant is usually bound to find and plant the trees as the old ones die off, being allowed the old tree for firing.
                    T.D. Acland and W. Sturge (1851)

The rural situation changed during the nineteenth century as capital and education became more available and farming enjoyed a prosperous period from 1840 to 1870. In Somerset, however, and particularly on the Levels, holdings remained fragmented and improvements were difficult to make although some landlords, like Robert Neville Grenville of Butleigh, began to take an increased interest in their farms, introducing steam engines and elaborate water

Delivering apples into the loft at Lower Ansford Farm, Castle Cary.

systems. But small farms remained the norm and, after the First World War, the opportunity given to many tenants to buy their land quite cheaply, coupled with a conservative farming tradition, helped to preserve the pattern and ensure the survival of small orchards.

Cider was needed by the farmer for his own social use, to provide part wages and refreshment through the working day for his regular labourers, and to sustain the temporary workforce at haymaking and harvest. To make the cider the farmer used a large wooden press and usually a wooden-framed apple mill. Although these pieces of equipment were cumbersome and expensive at fourteen guineas for a mill and £40 for a press, and fifteen guineas for the screws, gearings and fittings, they were not beyond the means of the nineteenth-century yeoman farmer or the skill of the local carpenter and blacksmith. Once bought they were a standing invitation to continue cidermaking.

Families often became attached to their cidermaking equipment and went to considerable efforts to keep it in good repair. When they moved they would sometimes try to take the equipment with them, though the fact that presses often support the building that they are in meant that this

Taking a break towards the end of building a cheese. Note the full square being used to shape it.

was often impossible, so the presses were left and can still be found although the more portable mills are rarer. When the machinery could be moved, the tradition of farmhouse cidermaking continued through generations of the family and various changes in location.

Most farms possessed a specially built ciderhouse or cellar. This was also called the wringhouse or poundhouse, and the best examples were carefully situated and insulated to maintain a cool, even temperature. The floor was usually cobbled although flagstones were laid in the wealthier late-Victorian farms.

Today the ciderhouse may still be shaded by a tree planted for this purpose while the roof is often insulated with straw and there are few windows. Above the cider cellar there is often an apple loft or tallet where the apples were stored before being stirred down through a hole in the floor to the mill below. Nowadays the lofts are rarely used as it is a laborious business carrying sacks to the higher storey and apples are generally milled as soon as they are collected, but the holes in the floor remain to indicate the original function of the loft.

Houses often have cellars where the cider was stored, if not made. The stone steps that lead to the cellar may be edged on either side with a smooth slope to facilitate the handling of casks; an example of this can be found at the Abbey Farm belonging to the Somerset Rural Life Museum at Glastonbury.

The cider cellar under a house at West Pennard.

Part of Thomas Escott's inventory.

An inventory of the goods of Thomas Escott, late of Sandhill near Withycombe, taken in November 1756, shows that the wringhouse was generally known there as the Hogshead Chamber. It contained at the time a cider press and apple mill worth £10 as well as various vats, tubs and empty casks. There were also two hogsheads of cider with six further hogsheads stored in the 'Cyderhouse'.

The ciderhouse provided the social focal point of the farm where labourers came to collect their daily ration of cider and where the ordinary visitor was entertained. On Saturday afternoons after wages had been collected, and on Sunday mornings, some ciderhouses became local meeting places rather like pubs. A few people earned themselves a Sunday drink by helping with the cidermaking.

In the eighteenth and nineteenth centuries cidermaking and brewing were part of the ordinary day-to-day work of the farm but more recently, within living memory, cider was more often made in the evening when the day's work was finished. An old barn, lit by candles with the reed and pomace glowing gold, was a sight to be remembered. Mr Adams, a boy in 1900, recalled 'the delight of sucking up apple juice direct from the cheese with a straw, hearing the rattle of the old mill, the squeak of the bearings'. Mr Meade remembered scouring the neighbourhood for cidermakings in the early twentieth century:

We used to go from place to place looking for the old hurricane lantern to see if they were making cider; and if we weren't pretty early we would probably not be able to get a turn on the handle that was grinding down the apples; so therefore we'd get there pretty early and wait and get a turn on the handle which entitled us to a piece of bread and cheese and some cider, which was something in those days.

CIDER AS WAGES

In the nineteenth century farm labourers were paid very little and cider was considered a part of the wages:

The labourer in a year takes off his master's hands about two hogsheads of cider and satisfies one of his bodily appetites at the cost of 15% of his earnings.
                    T.D. Acland and W. Sturge (1851)

In West Somerset the evidence accompanying Mr Boyle's report on the *Employment of Women and Children in Agriculture* (1867) shows that men were paid between 7s and 10s a week with several

Anticipation!

perquisites including, in most cases, cider valued at 1s. Most men preferred to take the cider rather than the extra shilling and it can be appreciated that it provided necessary refreshment for the body as well as maybe a little encouragement for the spirit through days of heavy work in all weathers.

Although of variable quality, cider was considered to be more reliable than the water in some parts. Farm labourers could not afford to be laid low by drinking polluted water during the thirsty days of harvest.

The amount of cider drunk varied with the weather and work; haymaking and harvesting involved long hours from five in the morning until ten at night and was hot and tiring. At this time the cider flowed freely, not only to quench the thirst but as an incentive to acquire the extra labour needed. Many farmers say that until the middle of this century you needed to have good cider to attract harvest labour. The usual allowance was two quarts a day for a man and one quart for a boy.

> *Throughout the year, on most farms, each labourer takes his half-gallon owl, or firkin, 'down in cellar' every morning to be filled, and during haymaking and harvest there is a double jorum.*
>
> *Cluster- O'-Vive*, John Read, 1923

Sometimes larger quantities were consumed. Mr Forshaw could remember taking out five and a half gallons in one day to two haymakers while Mr Brown said that the men who mowed with scythes used to drink half a gallon before breakfast.

The cider was taken into the fields in owls, firkins or jars. The owl, an apple shaped earthenware jar carried by a thong, is the oldest traditional container and rarely found today. A firkin is a small wooden cask which varies in capacity from half a pint to half a gallon: the smallest one was sometimes called a goose egg. These little casks, used by the youngsters and often bearing the owner's initials, were much loved and became family heirlooms. They were virtually a mark of manhood. A correspondent to the *Somerset County Herald* in 1939 remembered how proud he used to be when, going to plough, to 'see my little virkin hung on the horses' hames.'

Firkins were useful because they were nearly unbreakable but some people preferred the two-quart stone jars since they kept the cider cooler. The jars were liable to fracture and were therefore often cradled in basketwork to protect them.

A firkin, 11 inches high, which holds about half a gallon.

A stone jar enclosed in protective withies.

Stories are told of prodigious cider drinkers like the man who regularly drank three and half gallons a day. In 1824 the *Somerset Observer* recorded that a seventy-seven-year-old farmer at North Curry:

according to his own account has drunk on an average fourteen pints of cider daily for fifty years ... amounting to about five hundred hogsheads. He is now in perfect health, and has his usual daily allowance.

In noted feats two gallons were drunk without pausing for breath while nineteen pints were once downed in quick succession, but few people remember the usual level of cider drinking resulting in much drunkenness. Perhaps tolerance to cider was developed from an early age or hard work dissipated the effects, but on high days and holidays heavy drinking could pose a problem.

In the Middle Ages, Church Ales developed as social occasions intended to raise money for the church but these events became so disreputable that in 1596 Sir Francis Hastings left money to various churches in Somerset on condition:

that they never use again theyr churchales, to the prophaning of the Lorde's Sabaothe, the abusing of his creatures in dronkennes and ryott, and the corrupting of youth by trayning them up in gaminge and lascivious wantonnes and sundry other disorders.

Two hundred years later John Billingsley commented that it was not only the lower classes who had too much cider, 'but also the yeomanry themselves, who at times spend successive days and nights in toping and guzzling at each other's houses.'

In the twentieth century, particularly in times of economic hardship, some farmers drowned their sorrows in the cider butt; one wife in desperation pulled the bungs from the casks but demolished the remnants of family harmony in the process.

The wretched consequences of excessive cider drinking, and cider as wages, fuelled the powerful nineteenth-century temperance movement. Sir Thomas Dyke Acland was strong in his opposition to cider as wages: 'The liquor refreshes and stimulates him (the labourer) but wears him out, for common cider is not nourishing but exciting, like spirit and water. West Country labourers will never be what they might as long as this system goes on.' Sir Thomas did not give his labourers in West Somerset a cider allowance.

Some labourers were critical of the farmers' use of cider to placate their workforce. George Mitchell, a pioneer for agricultural workers' unions, addressed a meeting on Ham Hill, 'An' whet do 'em gi'? Zour Zider and chease and enuff to chuck a dorg!'

The cider provided for workman was often rough. George Saintsbury wrote in the 1860s:

...he gave me a truthful description of the horrible liquor which is given to the labourer under the ironical name of cider. For the labourers' cider windfalls are used ... or he has the second wringing ... and which can only be preserved by the addition of four gallons of hop-water to every hogshead, for without this addition it would, from its thinness and inferiority, turn to vinegar.

Quoted by a correspondent to the
Somerset County Herald, 3 May 1941

Cider truck was made officially illegal from 1887 but cider remained a necessary part of the relationship between a farmer and his men until the 1940s. Its popularity waned as machinery replaced horses, as farmers began to pay overtime and became more watchful of the time spent on, and the effects of, drinking cider, and as fewer farmers made cider themselves.

But cider was slow to disappear from holiday feasts. When the roistering Church Ales were abandoned, the Revel and later, the Club Day, took their place. On this day the farm labourers' friendly societies marched in procession to church and then to their annual feast. It was an occasion when food and cider were offered at various ports of call. W.G.W. Watson described a Club Day in *Somerset Life and Character*, 1924:

> *'Ees,' says Simeon, 'it do a man's hart good to zee varmer again on Club-day. I'll make a bet he's tapped th' best zider, that I will. Never had a better drop o' zider in m'life than that wur what he handed round last Club-walken.' Soon the cider-cups replenished by milking-pails, are in circulation, and everybody drinks to the health of measter and missus and the little uns.*

Club Days continued until early in the present century, when the successive introduction of pensions, national insurance and the National Health Service obviated the need for local friendly societies.

FARMHOUSE CIDER: VARIETIES AND RECIPES

Cider was offered generously to friends, neighbours and every visitor who came to the farm. One man, not a cider drinker, used to avoid walking through his neighbour's farmyard because he would be pressed to drink a mug of cider while at another farm the postman regularly called for his cider even if he had no letters to deliver. Nowadays farmers and their wives say they have so few visitors, for people no longer pass on foot and stop for a chat, that it is hardly worth making cider and anyway most would prefer a cup of tea or coffee.

Cider was sometimes used to smooth a deal; one old farmer remembered as a lad being told to keep the visitors' cups replenished; a special cask of good cider was kept for the 'toffs'.

Many people recall that cider was made in a number of qualities. The first cider of the season was often rather thin and colourless and did not keep so well as that made in November. It would be drunk quite quickly or handed to non-prestigious visitors like seasonal workers or tramps, though some people developed a liking for this sharp cider. One household had run out of cider when they were visited by a worker; the farmer said he was sorry but he had nothing to offer. The worker eyed a small cask in the kitchen and was told that the contents were cider vinegar, to which he replied that a drop of that would do! Rough cider has acquired some descriptive names such as tanglefoot and phlegm-cutter. Second-class cider would be drunk regularly by the farm workers and others for most of the year.

The best cider was specially blended from carefully selected apple varieties and made in cold weather. It was put into new brandy, rum or port casks and sometimes sultanas, raisins, sugar, lemons, ginger and other spices were added. It was really a cider wine and was made in the following way:

Cider Wine
To a gallon of apple juice add:
2lbs demerara sugar
3/4lb chopped raisins
1/2oz root ginger
1 stick of cinnamon
1 orange
  Mr & Mrs Boobyer

For 120 gallons the quantities become astronomical – and expensive:

 2 cwt sugar
 100 lemons
 40 lbs muscatel raisins
 root ginger
  Mr & Mrs Hecks

Mr and Mrs Hecks remembered the raisins vividly as they had minced them by hand in a kitchen mincer! Everyone agrees that the efforts were worthwhile and the drink was very fine. It was often made for the lady of the house and her friends. They preferred cider to tea in the mornings and it apparently made them 'very talkative'. Cider wine is not so common today but cider punch is still used for parties:

Cider Punch
3 gallons of cider
2 bottles orange cordial
2 bottles lemonade
2 lbs demerara sugar
2 teaspoons mixed spice
2 teaspoons ground ginger
For a more alcoholic drink, gin may be added. Serve hot or cold.
  Mrs Wilkins

Cider Punch
1 gallon of dry cider
2 pints new cider or apple juice
3 oranges, sliced 1 teaspoon nutmeg
1 teaspoon cloves
3-4 sticks cinnamon
2 pints gin
Warm thoroughly.
  Abbey Farm cidermaking punch

Gin and ginger are the most usual accompaniments for cider but Worlidge listed some other flavourings that were mixed in before fermentation including rosemary, wormwood, currants, raspberries, mulberries, blackberries, elderberries, and 'Clove-July Flower' which, dried and steeped in cider, gave an 'excellent tincture and flavour'. In 1810 Parsons said that some men 'to make more glad the hearts of their wives and neighbours, will not be content without putting brandy into their cider casks' but he did not like 'the devil muzzled' in this sort of way, or in any other.

Until the beginning of this century cider was occasionally distilled to produce apple-brandy (apple-jack). It never seemed to be very popular in Somerset, perhaps because a still was required. There was also a danger of producing methyl alcohol as the spirit is reduced from about thirteen times its quantity of cider. However, one family remembered apple-brandy being made at night by a man who carried the still on his back. It was hidden in stone jars in the farm pond.

Another account was given by Mr Meade:

Most people used to make it [Calvados] in my young days. They used to make it in the copper boiler or what they used to use for the clothes. Directly they had enough to fill the copper they used to rig up a pipe or apparatus or something where they could run off, or distil. The man who used to tell me about making it used to cover it down with clay after he put the cover on so the steam couldn't escape, only through the pipe. But I never remember tasting it but they told me they used to use it for veterinary medicines. I don't know whether that is right or not ... there was just a few that had some success – and when the German prisoners were over during the war they used to make all kinds of stuff; if they could they'd get cider. If they couldn't they'd make something with potatoes.

Cider was rarely used in cooking although one woman remembered a delicious pudding called New Cider Squash composed of layers of suet, new cider, mixed fruit, sugar and spices. It was cooked all day on the range and eventually served ceremonially with a large silver spoon.

The traditional food offered with cider was cider biscuits, also called tops and bottoms or hard bakes. They were usually made by the local baker and were a simple bread dough mixed with caraway seeds or lard and brown sugar, rolled flat and baked slowly to produce a rusk. The biscuits were cheap and often eaten as a simple, if not very nourishing, breakfast by Victorian workers.

Artefacts in Somerset County Museum

Photographs by Geoff Roberts

Horn cider beakers

Copper shoe for warming cider at the fireside

Milverton Young Men's Reform Benefit Society: cider jug and mugs

Cider mug presented to Mr William Hooper, born Feb. 28th, 1820

A cider owl, or hedgehog, made of earthenware, partly lead-glazed

Apples from local orchards ready for crushing at Perry's Cider Mills, Dowlish Wake

Using a traditional hand-powered apple mill, Kingston Apple Day 1997 Phil Stone

Building a straw cheese, Kingston Apple Day 1997
Phil Stone

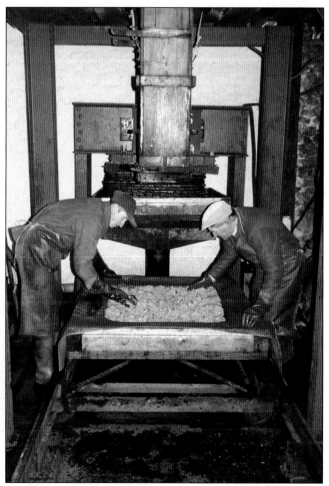

Building a cheese at Perry's Cider Mills, Dowlish Wake,
using cider cloths and racks

Sunrise over Old Cleeve community orchard, 1 May 1997 Jeanne Webb

Chapter 4
The Cider Business

'Maister; the zider do tuzzily!'

Until the 1930s, and in a few cases until the 1960s, it was common for farmhouses to sell cider. Sometimes it was sold at the door and for this no licence was required but when cider was made on a larger scale it became, in effct, a small business. In the early nineteenth century the Rev. Thomas Cornish planted orchards and started to make cider at Heathfield Rectory near Taunton. A story goes that he was preaching one day when the door of the church opened and a panting man ran in from the Rectory crying, 'Maister, the zider do tuzzily!' The Rector was soon out of the pulpit, onto his horse and galloping back to the Rectory. Presumably the cider was fermenting too fiercely, was 'tissing' or hissing and needed urgent attention!

By the 1840s, according to the cellar-book, the Rectory's customers included the Queen (one hogshead of prime cider), William Cavendish, the Carlton Club (two casks), Lord Rivers, the Duke of Bedford and the Bishop of Bath and Wells (one hogshead). The cider travelled to Cumberland, Dundee, Worcestershire, Yorkshire, Carlisle and many other places in Britain. The Spurway family continued the tradition; Edward Popham Spurway won a gold medal for his cider at the Bath and West Show in 1901. In about 1911 they lost their cider-maker, Arthur Moore, who, for an extra shilling a week, went to make cider for an enterprise at Norton Fitzwarren which eventually became the Taunton Cider Company, until recently part of Matthew Clark plc.

It was more usual for farms to sell their cider to local pubs. At the beginning of the twentieth century a large cider farm with about fifty acres of orchards at Stembridge sent two loads of cider every week to Yeovil and Chard, i.e. about 320 gallons. Other inns were also supplied and special orders for 'good strong cider' were sent to Wales and London. A rough computation shows that the farm made some 20,000 gallons a year and most of its income came from cider.

Cider was drunk by the ordinary working man because it was cheap, 1d or 1½d per pint against 3d per pint for beer. Many of the village pubs produced their own cider. The Hecks family of the Street Inn produced eighty hogsheads (4800 gallons) for their pub a year and the Meades, of the King's Head, Athelney, generally sold about one hogshead a week, with the occasional record sale of 120 gallons in three days. The Meades also supplied about twenty other inns. In the small villages publicans trusted their customers, even going to bed and leaving them to sit in the bar, knowing that the correct money would be put in the till if another drink was poured.

After the First World War medium-sized cider businesses suffered serious setbacks; brewers began to tie inns to their own cider production or a specially chosen cidermaker. If a cidermaker was to survive he had to make serious efforts to transport and market his product and in most cases neither finance nor expertise were available.

Cider drinking became less popular as money became more plentiful and people could afford other, more expensive, drinks. At the same time, many people in public houses had become used to their own farm cider from one particular farm with its own particular brew, and when they had to change over to a cider coming from the brewery it was not the same. 'There wasn't anything wrong, but it was different and as men had to change from the local cider which they understood and liked, a lot stopped drinking it,' said John Brown, once Senior Orchard Representative at R.N. Coates & Co Ltd, who was born in 1884.

A further complication for the small producer was a rise in the demand for table and culinary fruit and quite a number of cider apple trees were grafted over to Bramleys so that fewer cider apples were available. With the decline in interest in cider the existing orchards were often left to decay so the small maker found it more difficult to get enough apples, especially in a bad year.

These problems also affected the larger cider factories but were initially to their advantage; they took the apples off the hands of the farmers who were no longer making cider and in return the farmers received a few casks for their own consumption without the effort of making it. The factories were equipped with modern hydraulic presses which could dispose of large amounts of fruit very quickly. Clapps of Baltonsborough, who could put up forty-four cheeses in one day providing 5280 gallons of juice, made in the region of 260,000 gallons of cider in a good season. They must have worked very long hours. On two double-screw hand presses it would only be possible to put up six cheeses and extract about 800 gallons a day. Brakes of Nailsea, who used hand presses initially, produced 80,000 gallons of cider a year which were sold to pubs and clubs in Bristol and the surrounding area.

Clapps supplied local breweries such as Frome United Brewery, Georges of Bristol and Bristol United Breweries and for this had to pay a royalty. Their cider was bottled by Moons of Cardiff and Showerings of Shepton Mallet among others. They had their own bottling plant as well and produced a fine range of quality ciders.

Many of these producers started up just after the First World War but tied houses, brewery mergers, the 1930s slump, dwindling orchards and finally the Second World War saw the demise of most of them by the 1950s. A few survived, like the Taunton Cider Company which was chosen to supply the brewers, Brutton, Mitchell & Toms, who later became part of the Bass Charrington group. R.N. Coates & Co. Ltd of Nailsea adopted new methods and an energetic sales policy and was backed by sufficient capital to make it an attractive proposition to the Showering Group with which it merged in 1956. Showerings took over the Taunton Cider Company for a while and later Matthew Clark plc bought out Taunton Cider.

Smaller firms like Sheppys of Bradford-on-Tone and Perrys of Dowlish Wake survived by a mixture of luck,

Bob Clapp's cider factory, Baltonsborough, with the entire workforce in the 1930s.

energy and judgement. For example, at first the Perrys were also blacksmiths so had another source of income although this, too, was declining by the 1930s. They then began to make cider for local farmers, using local apples as well as some imported at first from Normandy. In the 1960s local supplies of apples started to improve, partly due to an initiative by Showerings, who encouraged the planting of new orchards, making contracts with farmers to take their apples and offering technical help. In recent years Perrys and Sheppys, like other firms, have benefited from the growing tourist trade, setting up museums or exhibitions of cidermaking and providing opportunities for visitors to watch cider being made. Tourists also make up a new market for cider, both scrumpy and the bottled ciders that are now available. All firms now produce a selection of good quality ciders in a variety of quantities.

The success of the cider business recently, both large and small companies, has inspired some new firms, perhaps with old family experience, to enlarge and become more scientific in their production. Small producers continue to attract a market at the gate of both local people and visitors, while other people like Alex Hill and Julian Temperley have entered the specialist market, producing sparkling cider by the *methode champanoise* and also cider brandy. Some families have turned back to cidermaking for their own social consumption, despite a lapse of a generation in the tradition.

Cider was once part of rural life in a way that it is unlikely ever to be again. It was one of the few pleasures of a working man's hard life but now other drinks and many other activities are within his reach. More fundamentally the close-knit rural community has broken up and most social occasions with cider as the main beverage have also disappeared. However it is interesting to note that as other alcoholic drinks become more expensive, people are returning to making cider for themselves and discovering just how good it can be.

As they make cider, sometimes alone, on a frosty night without the fun and friendship of former years, some present-day farmhouse cidermakers see themselves as the last of the line. But lights still shine out from sheds and barns on late autumn nights as people, anxious to learn the skills and knowledge of their forebears, continue the tradition of cidermaking in Somerset.

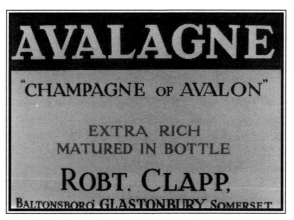

Cider bottle label.

Chapter 5
Making Cider: Equipment

An apple mill and press had been erected on the spot, to which some men were bringing fruit from divers points in mawn-baskets, while others were grinding them, and others wringing down the pomace, whose sweet juice gushed forth into tubs and pails.
The Woodlanders, Thomas Hardy

The two major pieces of cidermaking equipment are the mill or 'crusher' which breaks up the apples, and the cider press which extracts the juice. Until the nineteenth century, and even then only occasionally, these machines were rarely dated or stamped with the maker's name. Consequently it is difficult to date equipment accurately although it is possible to work out a sequence in its development.

THE CIDER MILL

Somerset is unusual among cidermaking counties in possessing few of the old circular stone mills. These mills each consisted of a circular stone trough in which apples were placed to be crushed by a massive stone wheel turned by a horse. One farm in the north of the county once had an unused and incomplete stone mill in the garden, the stone apparently dressed at Nailsea, but the mill was transported to Gloucestershire and only later returned to Somerset as a family heirloom.

It is possible that a curved wooden trough in which a stone was rolled back and forth was an early form of

mill in Somerset but none have been found here, although a specimen from Herefordshire can be seen at the Museum of Cider in Hereford.

Early writers like Worlidge described apples being pounded in such troughs. '[It was the custom] for the Operators to beat their Fruit in a Trough of Wood or Stone with Beaters like unto Wooden Pestles with long handles.' Worlidge recognised that the method was slow and inconvenient for it required the work of three or four servants to process 20 to 30 bushels of apples in a day, or enough for a single cheese. He therefore set to and invented the 'Ingenio' which could grind five to eight bushels in an hour, requiring just two men to turn the wheels. The main body of the

Ingenio mill illustrated in *Vinetum Britannicum.*

machine was wood with heavy fly-wheels. The first model had a single cylinder with 'pegs of iron' which broke up the apples. An improved design had a pair of rollers '... about 8 or 10 inches in Diameter, and about ten inches in length; Let the Teeth be about two Inches, or two Inches and a half distance so that they be able to take in an Apple of Ordinary size ... Let the teeth be bellying out or rounding so that in turning, the Rolls may Shute even in every place alike.'

These fluted rollers or jambs remained basic to the design of many apple mills until the end of the nineteenth century. No mills of the 'Ingenio' type with the wooden fly-wheels have yet been found in Somerset but there are a number of examples possessing one fly-wheel.

From observation it seems that the earlier mills of the eighteenth century tended to have sloping pomace troughs and were made of stout timber with beading along one edge. Some mills from this period are tall, rising to the first floor so that the apples could be pushed straight from the loft into the hopper. Because of their height these mills could not be operated by hand and so were driven by a rotating shaft from a horse-gin. Two fine examples of this system have been found in Somerset, and in one the horse-gin bears the date 1774. The wooden structured horse-gin continued to be used until the early twentieth century although in many places it was replaced by a much more compact cast-iron gin. Some farms still have a round house where the docile pony circled. The horse-gear powered other farm machinery as well as apple mills.

By the beginning of the nineteenth century the small pegged or fluted rollers were supplemented by a pair

A wooden horse gin from Curry Rivel. The horse turned the wheel, the wheel the cog, and the cog the rollers of the apple mill.

of large lower rollers, between 14 and 18 inches in diameter, made of elm or oak. Later in the century some were made from granite or pennant, a local hard stone from North Somerset. These stone rollers were more expensive.

The earlier examples of double-roller mills, those that still possess a massive wooden wheel, often have cogs set into the lower rollers. This feature is surprising since the pomace might well have clogged the workings which may account for its disappearance by the end of the nineteenth century. Wooden wheels were eventually discarded in favour of cast iron.

From the 1850s various experiments were made to improve the cutting power of the upper rollers. These led to the 'scratter mill' in which two small cast-iron

A single wooden wheel mill similar to Worlidge's 'Ingenio'.

An apple mill by Albert Day of Mark made in 1880.

rollers were matched with interlocking pegs and sockets. A man who had used both a fluted roller mill and a scratter mill said the scratter was far more efficient. It was this type of mill that was made by Albert Day of Mark in Somerset.

Denings of Chard retained the fluted rollers but added, in some models, lower granite rollers. They

also developed a sturdy but elegant iron frame. Some of the later Day Mills also had iron frames. The larger makers produced a variety of machines at different prices and for different purposes. The double wheels of hand operated mills were often adapted on one side for water or engine power.

In 1890 a trial of cider machinery was held at

Glastonbury. Unfortunately there were only three competitors. Both the Dening and Workman mills operated at approximately the same speed, grinding one hundred pounds of apples in about a minute and

An apple mill by John Smith at Broadway.

a quarter. The Dening mill broke on a stone and the other entry was very slow. The Workman mill, which received the prize, had only one top roller made of wood set with wrought-iron studs that revolved 250 times per minute in close apposition to a horizontal metal plate, a design rather similar to Worlidge's original 'Ingenio'. It was enhanced by a wooden plunger that regulated and pressed the flow of apples to the roller. The lower rollers were made of pennant stone. Workman and Sons were still producing similar mills in 1927 but by the 1930s high speed grater mills were replacing the traditional mill designs that had served well for two centuries.

THE CIDER PRESS

The first reference to a cider press in Somerset occurs in 1230, when the Bishop of Bath received a grant referring to the use of cider presses. Unfortunately they were not described but were obviously notable machines.

Worlidge compared various types of press. Of screw presses he said there were some 'very large, that a Hogshead may be pressed at once; and as some report, that a Hogshead or two runs out commonly before the Apples suffer any considerable pressure ... Some of these large Skrew-presses are made of two Skrews, and some of but one.' The press and screws were made entirely of wood and were expensive. He recommended a basket press but preferred the flail press because it pressed the cheese slowly. Examples of single wooden screw presses have been found in Somerset. Very few are complete but where a press is tall or heavy or slightly decorated with beading or moulding in some way, it is worth checking the top beam to see if there is an early screw-hole about ten

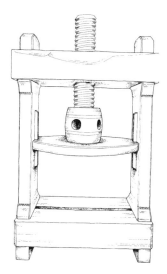

A single wooden screw press with central wooden boss, Southwood, near Glastonbury.

the other. A beam press at Chew Stoke is raised and lowered by a complex system of cog-wheels which may be a later adaptation.

The introduction of cast-iron screws in the mid-eighteenth century revolutionised the construction of presses. Initially the wooden screws and bosses were replaced by iron parts of similar dimensions, the single metal screw being 4 to 5 inches in diameter. As technology advanced, changes were made, the screws became smaller, 2½ to 3 inches, and the boss was replaced by a lugged turning-wheel. The pole was made of iron and formed into a semi-circular shape at the end to lock round the central nut. The single presses were often attached to a capstan or windlass to help put pressure on the cheese. 'In the morning the press is strained as tight as it will bear by a level or cap-staff,' commented John Billingsley.

inches in diameter. If there is, the press is probably pre-1750. The mechanics are simple – a pole is turned in the central boss to raise and lower the drift beam onto the cheese.

The flail press appears to operate on the same system as a screw press, but was probably cheaper because the screw is replaced by a toothed iron bar which is moved by the action of the 'flail' wheel. This could be weighted to leave the press in the required position. Another primitive form of press is the beam press. These are common in France but more unusual in Britain. Three are known to exist in Somerset. The presses are rather low and long with two base beams set some distance apart and a moving top beam. Two varieties are illustrated in the *Encyclopaedia Britannica* for 1768 to 1797. The massive timbers were often moved by a screw on one end and a pegged plate at

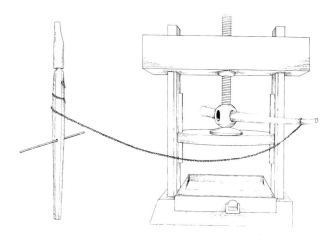

Single iron screw press with central boss and capstan, Panborough.

A double screw press with large cog wheels, Burcott, near Wells.

Double-screw presses became increasingly popular since large cheeses could be built on the bed and the two screws provided a more even distribution of pressure. The primitive versions do not have a drift beam, the turning-wheels are positioned on top of the summer (top beam) and can only be wound down. The summer is then hauled back using a pulley and windlass; in some cases a massive wooden wheel is situated in the roof above the press to assist this process.

A more advanced model incorporates a nut and bolt system on the screw and a collar joins the beam to the

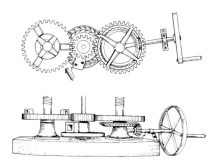

Detailed drawing of the working of the double screw ratchet press at Wedmore.

nut so the beam can be wound down and up. Various turning mechanisms are found although all use a pole or press-bar. One version has become known as a 'ramshorn press' because of the extended curving metal bars that lock the pole. These are possibly an early form since one is known to have been in existence before 1842.

Double-screw presses posed a problem since care had to be taken to keep the beam level. There are one or two examples of gear-wheels linking huge turning-

Workman and Sons' worm-geared press at East Lambrook.

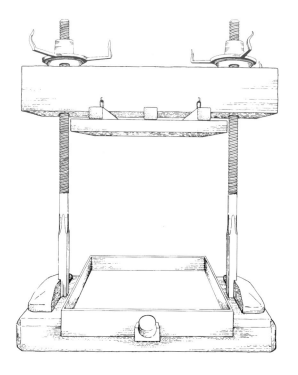

A ramshorn press at North Perrott.

A triple screw press: details of screws and gears at Bury, near Dulverton.

A travelling cidermaker's equipment from the Dulverton area. The geared unit fixed to the right-hand side of the press is a hand-powered mill. Note, too, the long ash pole for applying extra force to the screws.

44

wheels on the screws above the summer but the idea was improved by reintroducing a drift beam and linking the screws at that level. The next step was to eliminate the effort required to return the drift beam after pressing and to simplify the press-bar procedure, so a simple ratchet and further gears were added. Presses of this last type were made by Workman & Sons of Slimbridge and won the R.A.S.E. prize in 1890. Although the Workman and Dening presses produced virtually the same amount of juice the Workman press took a third of the time.

Travelling presses were made in Somerset by Days and by Denings. Workmans also made them, but very few of any make have been found in Somerset, as there were usually enough presses in a neighbourhood to make a travelling press unnecessary.

THE CIDER MACHINERY MAKERS

Since so few of the mills and presses are named and dated, particularly those made before 1850, many makers will remain unknown. In some villages the similarity of the machines is so striking that it indicates local workmanship. For example, the area around North Curry possesses a number of double-screw presses with a non-returnable summer lifted by a windlass located on the side of the press.

Screws and attachments for presses were sold separately. In 1856 Oliver Maggs of Bourton Foundry, Dorset, and Wincanton, Somerset, advertised 'a pair of 2¾ inch Wrought Iron Cider Screws with Drawing Arms, Boxes and Followers' for £9. For a 'single 4 inch Cast Iron Cider Screw, with Bore and Follower', the charge was £2. By 1863 the firm has been taken over by E.S. Hindley and he offered a double-screw metal frame press in which 'the two screws are coupled with gearing' for £30. With wooden head and base pieces the price was £22. It was probably quite usual for a local carpenter to provide the woodwork needed to complete the press. One complication in the dating of machinery is the possibility of the local man reproducing a tried and approved design for some thirty or fifty years ignoring all innovations.

The Victorian enthusiasm for machinery and the new iron technology led to a proliferation of iron foundries. Edward Murch of Bridgwater (later Murch and Spence) employed thirty men in 1853 and won the prize at the Bath and West Show for a 'well constructed iron mill'. Only one mill made by this firm has so far been located in Somerset.

The firm of Wightman & Dening of Chard (later Messrs Dening & Co.) was founded in 1828 and became a large company making a variety of agricultural implements – they made a whole range of mills and presses. In 1883 it was noted that their apple mill was very similar to one they had displayed in 1856.

Messrs John Smith & Co., also of Chard, made very distinctive apple mills on iron frames with tall hoppers. They also made cider presses but none has been found with a name plate. Dening and Smith mills and presses are found in the south and west of Somerset but in the central and northern areas machines made by Day, Wensley or Knapton are more common.

Albert Day and James Wensley both lived in the village of Mark. Day was a blacksmith turned ironfounder who employed fourteen men in 1871. Wensley, a younger man, was originally a master carpenter. There may well have been some association

Name plate on a Wensley mill at Burrowbridge.

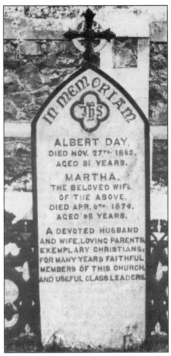

The gravestone of Albert Day, ironfounder, of Mark.

between the two men because the mills they produced were very similar. They both put name-plaques on the mills but only Day dated them. They were individually represented at the Bath and West Show in 1883. Day made oak and iron-framed mills. Very occasionally presses were found with 'Day and Wensley' plaques. Eli Knapton of Huntspill also began as a carpenter but by 1866 he was described as a smith and wheelwright. One apple mill of his is dated 1859.

Some names occur only occasionally. Rowe of Hewish made the wheels and possibly the rest of a travelling press in about 1860. Lovell & Wright of Glastonbury presented an apple mill for £10 at the Bath and West Show in 1856. W. & J. Naish of West Pennard made an iron horse-gear. The name J. & J. Talbott of Yeovil appears on the cast-iron gear-wheels of a couple of mills. Lang & Culverwell have name plates on mills of the Day/Wensley type – it is possible they were agents rather than makers.

One unusual press was dated 1857 and labelled W.H. Pool. Pool was an inventor and mechanical engineer in the Chipstable area and he and his sons were famous for their variety of agricultural tools and range of small oil-engines. His press was a geared double-screw with a centrally placed handle for quick raising and lowering.

It is unfortunate that only some machinery makers were of sufficient size to publish catalogues or advertise and that only a few of those survive. As a result our knowledge of their work is limited.

Chapter 6
Making Cider: Processes

The procedure for making farmhouse cider is essentially simple. Ripe apples are milled, pressed, and the juice extracted. The juice is put into clean wooden casks with few or no additives and left to ferment. After an initial violent fermentation the barrel is 'bunged down' tightly and left for a period of one to five months, or longer, before it is drunk, depending on weather, apple varieties and need.

In detail, however, there is a lot to learn and an old cidermaker will have a fund of knowledge and experience which may die with him. Some of the secrets of the trade have been lost over the centuries while others have been periodically rediscovered. Cidermaking methods have always been open to debate and many writers have criticised the general standard:

...neither doth one in ten of substantial Housekeepers in the greatest part of the Nation make, or scarce know how to make this Drink ... Thus hath this liquor been undervalued by the ignorant, which did prevent a long time many from understanding its improvement.
John Worlidge, 1676

The condition and sort of apples are of primary importance. The apples should be tested for ripeness by pushing a thumb firmly across the skin of the apple and if it punctures easily, the apples are ready. Black rotten apples are better removed, although brown rotten ones are acceptable in reasonable quantities. The apples should be free of twigs and leaves although most cidermakers think it undesirable to wash the fruit. It was thought for many years that the yeasts necessary for fermentation were found on the skins of the apples but this is now considered unlikely and it is thought that they actually lodge in the equipment and ciderhouse. The mix of apples used for each cheese should be well balanced and for present-day taste this is about 75% bittersweets and the rest sweets and sharps. If the balance is incorrect the cider can taste too sharp, have little body or be a poor colour.

The apples are milled into small pieces, which retain their juice, by a machine powered by hand, horse or engine. At this stage uncooked beetroot may be milled to add colour to the cider. Blackberries and elderberries were also used as colourings. The apple pieces are termed 'pomace' or 'pummy' and collect in a wooden 'bow' under the mill. This is generally made of elm, as John Worlidge pointed out: 'a square Chest made long and deep, of Elme well jointed'.

Traditionally everything that came into contact with cider was made of wood since metals, especially iron,

Milling fruit by hand, probably early this century. Note the wooden shovel leaning against the mill.

[It is] highly injurious to the nerves, hence it suppresses the natural intestinal discharges, producing obstinate costiveness, and a peculiar species of collick terminating in palsy of the extremities, which generally deprives them of motion, without destroying their sensation.

According to William Marshall in 1796, this was not the only problem. The poor sufferer, resorting to badly distilled apple brandy for cure, could also be affected by methyl alcohol poisoning. Once these facts were known, metal was avoided in cidermaking although copper dippers and funnels are found quite often.

The apple pomace was transferred to the press using a wooden shovel or 'scoop'. Today this is done as soon as the apples are ground but Worlidge described the old process of maceration: ' 'tis good to let it stand twenty-four or forty-eight hours ... in large vessels ... where it starts to ferment and acquires colour.' In the twentieth century this process was investigated at Long Ashton Research Station and was found to increase the pectin and pectase contents of the juices which made effective the subsequent process of 'keeving' described on page 51.

All the equipment used for cidermaking should be thoroughly cleaned before use as one cidermaker commented in 1810: '... through the whole process observe cleanliness above all things.' The 'bed' or 'dish' of the press has to be prepared first since it must not leak. It is 'primmed up' by blocking the spout and filling any cracks with clay or 'wool and cow dung'. Water is poured in and the wood swells until it is completely watertight and then the temporary fillers can be scrubbed out.

dissolve and taint the cider. The most notorious example of this happened in the eighteenth century when Devonshire Colic was identified as lead poisoning, caused by using lead to repair cider machinery and by adding 'sugar of lead' to sweeten the cider. Dr Fothergill warned of the dangers in 1790 and described the symptoms:

Building a straw cheese using the traditional longstraw method with the layers or lissoms clearly visible. Probably at Manor Farm, Limington, in 1934.

The next process is to construct the 'cheese' or 'setting' on the bed. In Somerset this is usually done with straw or 'reed'. Reed is combed wheat straw, about four feet long, although some people prefer oat straw. These reeds were also called 'liners'. It is vital that the straw is clean and sweet otherwise it will taint the cider. Horsehair cloths were more common than reed in the north of the county and were used until the 1940s. The pomace was enveloped, layer by layer, in these strong, coarse cloths. Unfortunately they were expensive, heavy and difficult to clean; one cidermaker remembered scrubbing them out on the road when it was underwater in the floods of 1929. They were discarded in favour of cotton, and then nylon and polyester cloths.

There are two basic methods of constructing a straw cheese. In the first the liners are laid neatly east/west and north/south across the bed, leaving a gap of about 4 to 6 inches between the reed and the edge of the bed. The pomace is placed on top leaving the ends of the liners sticking out from the cheese. The corners are made using an 'half square' which is placed at each corner in turn. When the pomace reaches a level of about 4 inches, more liners are placed, as before, on top. Thus a layer, 'lissom' or 'cake' of the cheese has been formed. The next lissom is made slightly smaller than the first. A cheese can consist of some eight to twelve lissoms and is slightly pyramidal in shape.

The second method is carried out using liners of baled straw and consequently is more common today since reed is rare and expensive. A full square or 'frame' is used to form the lissom. Straw is placed in the square and the pomace piled in. The straw is pulled up the sides and pummelled down into the pomace. In the old days the reed was twisted before it was tucked in. The square is then raised and held in place by hazel spars while the next lissom is built. This cheese rises straight, or should!

Making a cheese is quite an art and is the task of the most experienced cidermaker present. If it is uneven or insecure it is much more likely to split under pressure and an evening's work is wasted. When the cheese has reached the required height a heavy square of timber called a 'vollyer' or 'hatch' is laid on top to disperse the pressure, further weight is usually added in the form of blocks of wood, sometimes called 'plocks'. Then the drift beam or summer, depending on the type of press, is brought down to rest on the timbers. At this point most makers leave the cheese for 12 hours, or overnight, to settle. The reasons given,

A double screw press showing plocks in place to weight the cheese, Minehead area.

The speed of the pressing depends on the requirements of the farmer or cidermaker. When he has other tasks and the crop of apples is light, a cheese could stay for a week being pressed gradually. The edges of the cheese are trimmed, often with a hay-knife, the shearings placed on top and the cheese pressed again; generally a cheese can be pressed fairly thoroughly over two days.

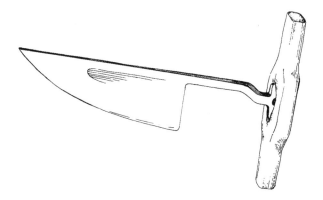

A hayknife used to trim the cheese after the first pressing; the one necessary exception to the rule about metal not coming into contact with the pulp or juice.

apart from 'enough is enough for one evening', are that it is unwise to press too quickly as the cheese may break, and also the juice acquires a better colour from apples left to stand.

Very few cidermakers follow any other process with the juice except to pump or pour it into casks. Before the widespread use of pumps the juice was scooped out of the trough with a large wooden bowl or 'dipper' and put into wooden pails or buckets. In some cases it was carried perhaps 200 yards to the cellar, where it was poured into the casks through a wooden funnel called a 'tundish' or 'tunnacre'. However, Worlidge recommended that the juice be put into a large vat with a cloth over it, and Marshall

A wooden cider dipper in Somerset Rural Life Museum.

recounted that cider was 'placed in large vessels or cisterns, for its feculences to subside, before it is put into casks.' Parsons in 1810 gave full instructions:

Then take the first running, the virgin cider as it is called, and put it in an open cask, commonly called a kieve, and cover it with a hair cloth or bag, to accelerate the first saccharine fermentation; and let this be a standing rule for your first racking from the kieve, namely to set about it when the thick red head or crust which covers the cider ... begins to separate and white bubbles appear.

Only in western Somerset is any process of this kind remembered today. The juice is left overnight and the floating particles skimmed off with a cream skimmer. This may be a relic of keeving but the process is well known in France and was used by Neville Grenville at the turn of the century. When keeving was studied at

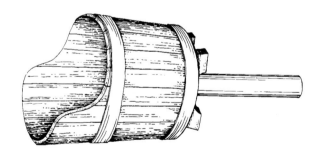

A tunnacre or tundish.

A cane cider strainer.

51

Long Ashton it was found that a thick, brown jelly head was formed on the juice. As a result the soluble nitrogen content of the juice was reduced and it fermented slowly and stopped before all the sugars were absorbed, leaving a naturally sweet cider that 'dropped bright'. Perhaps this was the method used at Briddicott Farm, Carhampton, where their bright cider was known as champagne cider.

This enviable result is rarely achieved in farmhouse cidermaking and many things have been recommended to remedy cider that does not turn out so well. Ribs of beef certainly have been added for the cider to 'feed on'. In 1837 the *Taunton Courier* reprinted an item which suggested that two or three pairs of calves' feet should be suspended in the cask as the animal jelly helped clear the cider.

Worlidge recommended isinglass instead of racking as a way of ensuring clarity in the juice and 'wheat, eggs, figges or sugar' as a means of curing acidic cider, which in Somerset is described as 'summery'. Sugar was occasionally used as a sweetener but more often for colouring. It was boiled until black in a large crock and then, at the critical moment, boiling water was poured on to it, the mixture frothed violently and it was added to the cask.

In a recipe book dating from the 1820s a farmer's wife included remedies for cider that was giving anxiety. To 'thin cider' she added 2lbs of rice and ½lb hops per two hogsheads, and to 'cider that is turning off, mash a few parsnips, cut off the tops and bottoms, put them in the cask.'

Water has sometimes been added to cider and although this practice is generally censured it was possibly once common. In some cases water-cider, or 'ciderkin' as it was sometimes called, was acceptable. It was made from soaking pressed pomace in water and re-pressing. The beverage was:

... for the common drinking of Servants, Etc., supplying the place of Small-beer and to many more agreeable.

Sylas Taylor, Evelyn's *Pomona*.

Cider is subject to a number of disorders. It can turn thick and viscous when it is called 'oily' or contain long, thread-like organisms when it is called 'ropey'. Violent agitation of the cask and proper use of sodium metabisulphite may cure this condition but earlier writers suggested mustard as a remedy. 'Mothery' is a term applied to cider affected by acetic acid bacteria when a stringy brown mass is formed. The best way of preventing this is to make sure cider does not come into contact with the air.

It has long been known that sulphur compounds will counteract some of the unwanted bacteria in cider and that it will be less acidic as a result. Dr Beale thus described the method of 'matching' or 'slumming' cider in 1657:

So some do lay Brimstone on a Rag and by a wire let it down into the cider vessel and there fire it; and when the vessel is full of smoak, the liquor speedily poured in ferments the better.

This practice is remembered by a present-day cidermaker although he no longer uses it. He recalled that when you pulled the cork out of the cask after matching, it went 'boohm!' Parsons disliked all additives, and advised:

A sugar-burning crock in Somerset Rural Life Museum.

In Somerset, most of the casks are, or were, acquired through the Port of Bristol and new sherry, port, rum, whisky and brandy casks are highly prized – beer barrels are not suitable. For the first year or two the original contents will impart a flavour to the cider.

The most common cask in Somerset is the tall port 'pipe' holding between 110 and 120 gallons, the sherry 'butt' holding the same amount but a shorter, fatter cask, and the traditional hogshead holding 54 gallons. The Hereford hogshead holds about twice that amount. The 42-gallon whisky cask is also found, as is the three-hogshead cask. There are one or two 300-gallon casks about but these seem to have been specially made. Casks are usually made of oak, although chestnut is sometimes used. As the wooden ones become rare they are replaced by plastic containers, which are efficient but have no charm. The casks are generally laid on their sides and in that way another row can be laid on top. Some are kept upright, particularly if the head seal is not as good as it used to be. Casks are laid on wooden 'horsing' to keep them off the ground.

Have nothing to do with brimstone, sugar of lead, burnt sugar, parched wheat, burnt beans, spirit of nitre, isinglass, bullock's blood, and the rest of the trumpery prescribed by cider quacks.

Every cidermaker insists that sound, sweet casks are essential to good cider:

It hath been no small occasion of the badness of this Liquor, and thereby giving it an ill name, that it hath been usually ill-treated, and entertained (after it hath been indifferently well made) in ill shaped, corrupt, faulty and unsound vessels.

Worlidge

The cooper's craft of making and repairing casks has virtually died out but cidermakers still speak of the craftsman with great respect, especially in the Wedmore area of Cooper Thomas, 'a wonderful man with barrels ... he would cycle out with his little bag of tools; he was only a little man but he had that knack of being able to handle the big barrels.' (Mr Rose). He charged little for his work and would make pails and tundishes from old staves for about 4s 6d.

When a cask was empty it was scrubbed out and left to dry; sometimes a chain was turned in the cask to help dislodge the lees. Clapp's cider factory had a special barrel washing machine since 'if you neglect

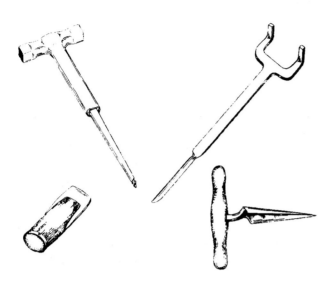

Tools for the care of casks: bung extractor, drift, rushing iron and borer.

Once the cider is in a sound cask it is left to ferment in a cool cellar, the slower the fermentation the better. For one to four weeks it froths from the bunghole, which is left open. Every day the cask is topped up to prevent air entering. When the froth subsides and the cider cannot be heard to hiss strongly, it is 'bunged down', lightly at first and then firmly. If this is done too soon the bung can be blown out and a large quantity of cider lost.

Many small cidermakers leave the cider on the lees but others 'rack off' into another cask. This may be done twice, early in the fermentation and before drinking; very few makers will rack as frequently as Parsons did: 'you must give it six or seven rackings within the first five or six weeks.' However Parsons was going to bottle his cider and this has always needed more care. At the beginning of the twentieth century, and perhaps before, the best cider was sent to a factory or wine merchants where it was bottled and became a sparkling drink for special occasions. Bulmers and Neville Grenville experimented with the champagne method which produced a fine cider, but it was skilled and time-consuming work and the process was replaced later by carbonisation.

your barrels you might as well finish cidermaking' (Mr Redman). One way of trying to rescue a musty cask was to burn it out; straw was fired in the cask which was then rolled around. It only had to be burnt 'a nice nut-brown', no charcoal, and you had to be very quick to stop the fire getting a hold. Generally it was better to break up a musty cask for firewood or use the staves around apple trees as a livestock guard.

It is important to remember that each cidermaker will produce a distinctive cider which is liable to some changes due to the weather and availability of apple varieties. The local brew and method will be defended by regular drinkers as the only one worth having!

Chapter 7
Folklore

Let every man take off his hat
And shout out to the old apple tree!
                    Carhampton Wassail Song

By the middle of the twentieth century most folk customs associated with cider and apple trees had disappeared. Only a few people today remember wassailing apple trees although the activity continued in Walton until the early 1970s and is still carried on each year at Carhampton. It was revived for a while by the Taunton Cider Company at Norton Fitzwarren.

The word 'wassail' comes from the Anglo Saxon 'waes hael' meaning 'health be to you' and the ceremonies developed from the wish of people to ensure good health and prosperity to people, stock and crops while celebrating with songs, food and drink. In 1686 John Aubrey recorded the practice in Somerset on 'Twelve Eve':

> *... the ploughmen have their Twelve-cake, and they go into the Oxhouse, to the oxen with the Wassell-bowl and drink to the ox with crumpled horn, that treads out the corne; they have an old concerved rhythme: and afterwards they goe with their Wasselbowle into the orchard and goe about the trees to blesse them, and putt a piece of tost upon the roots in order to it.*

The ceremonies vary a little from place to place. At Walton on 17 January (Old Twelfth Night), the wassailing cup was filled with a mixture of hot cider, gin and ginger at the village pub and passed around the assembled crowd. For such an important occasion a special cup was used and the Walton one still exists and is particularly fine; it holds about three quarts and has three handles. Everyone went to an orchard and gathered around an old tree. A piece of toast soaked in cider was put into its branches for the good spirits and a wassailing song was sung.

> *Old apple tree we wassail thee*
> *And happily thou wilt bear,*
> *For the Lord doth know where we shall be*
> *Till apples another year.*
> *To bloom well and to bear well*
> *So merry let us be,*
> *Let every man take off his hat*
> *and shout out to th'old apple tree:*
> *Chorus: (shouted)*
> *Old apple tree! we wassail thee!*
> *And hoping thou would bear.*
> *Hatsful, capsful, dree bushel bagsful*
> *And a little heap under the stair*
> *Hip, hip, hooray!*
> *Hip, hip, hooray!*
> *Hip, hip, hooray!*

Carhampton Wassail Song

Carhampton Wassail Night, 17 January 1979. Firing shotguns into the trees to frighten away evil spirits.

A shotgun was then fired through the branches of the tree in order 'to frighten away the evil spirits.' At nearby Walton a pile of apples and a jar of cider were placed beneath the tree while the crowd processed round the orchard. These festivities were followed by a venison supper at the local pub, although on one notable occasion the venison was replaced by badger.

Wassailling at Walton in the 1950s.

Wassailing in the more general sense of singing for Christmas good cheer and refreshment is all part of ciderdrinking in the West Country and is still found in the villages of Drayton and Curry Rivel on 5 January (Old Christmas Eve). Thomas Hardy recounted how the wassailers would expect to be rewarded for their efforts:

'Neighbours, there's time enough to drink a sight of drink now afore bedtime?' said Mail. 'True, true – time enough to get drunk as lords!' replied Bowman cheerfully.

In Somerset the wassail song used included these two verses:

The ashen faggot ceremony at the King William IV inn at Curry Rivel in the 1960s.

Wassail and wassail, all over the town,
The cup it is white, and the cider it is brown.
The cup it is made of the good old ashen tree,
And so is the malt of the best barley.
For its your wassail, and its our wassail
And its joy be to you, and a jolly wassail.

There was an old man, and he kept an old cow
And how for to keep her he didn't know how,
He built up a barn for to keep his cow warm,
And a drop or two of cider will do us no harm.
No harm, boys, harm. No harm, boys, harm.
And a drop or two of cider will do us no harm.

Cider, as a drink so easily available, was part of many festivities. On new or old Christmas Eve an ashen faggot was often burnt. In most of Somerset this custom died out with the First World War although in the more remote districts of Exmoor it took two world wars to extinguish it. The faggot was made by collecting a bundle of long ash twigs, about 5 feet in length and sometimes twisted like a figure-of-eight; it was important to tie as many bonds as possible around the bundle since when each one broke in the fire another mug of cider was passed round. The death blow to this custom was struck when small contained fireplaces replaced the great open hearths, but in some cases the ashen faggot was just made smaller.

Ash is often thought to have magical properties and it is interesting to note that ash cups and faggots are connected with cider; it was recorded that some farmhouses kept the last unburnt ash stick from the faggot and put it in the cowstalls to bring good luck in rearing calves in the following year. The stick was then used to light the next year's faggot. On the other hand it was thought on Exmoor that an apple tree should not be planted near an ash or mountain ash as one would kill the other.

Some towns in Somerset held 'Ashen Faggot Balls'. That held in Taunton on 2 January 1826 was 'most respectably attended by the principal families of the town and neighbourhood'. It was still an annual event twenty years later, but by then was losing its appeal.

Another custom that has died out is that of cider-drinkers tipping a few drops of cider on to the floor after drinking. John Read records a similar practice when the cider starts to run from the press:

Jonas held out at arms' length a brimming cup of old cider and with a movement of his wrist as gentle as the opening of a butterfly's wings made the immemorial libation. 'A drop for the wold Heark!' he said, and the cup made the round.

Cluster-O'-Vive, 1923

This is possibly all that remains of an ancient offering to the world spirit or goddess of fruit trees – but it would not be met with much enthusiasm in public houses today!

Most of the active events associated with cider happen at Christmastide but the middle of May (19, 20, 21) is an important time for the apple trees since then they are usually in flower or just setting fruit. A frost at this time could be disastrous to the crop. In Somerset a story is recorded, although no one seems to remember it now, of how St Dunstan bought some barley to make beer and in order to have a market for his brew made a pact with the Devil to destroy the apple crop – thus the cold easterly gale which frequently occurs on St Dunstan's Day (19 May). This story is particularly surprising since St Dunstan is said to have been born at Baltonsborough, in the heart of great apple country, so his wish to brew beer seems most unlikely!

Two superstitions relating to cidermaking are that the youngest person present should be the first to drink the new juice from the press, and the first cidermaking of the season should not happen on a Friday.

Cider is a stronger drink than some believe, sometimes twice the strength of beer, and as a result there are many stories relating to its effects upon the unwary visitor or tourist. One family used to lay bets as to whether the visitor would make it to the bridge on their land about 400 yards away; others can remember brave attempts to ride off on bicycles that ended painfully in the hedge. When people travelled by horse and cart a favourite trick was to unhitch the horse from the cart while the driver drank a few pints and re-hitch the horse with its traces through some railings. The driver would blithely attempt to drive off, but to no avail. One woman recalled a wet day when her small nieces and nephews were sent off to play in the barn. Hours later they reappeared, walking haphazardly, saying, 'Oh, Granpa's cider makes us feel so happy!' The most terrible tale is of a man who drank some brandy, or too much cider, and fell asleep in a cask. The cask was inadvertently filled up with

Reveller on the annual feast day of Barrington Friendly Society, 1907.

60

cider and when re-opened revealed only his ring and the bottle, all the rest being 'ait up by the cider'.

Other animals fell in, or were perhaps put in – poultry, mice and rats being the most common. One story concerned a barrel at the Rodney Stoke Inn. When it was emptied for cleaning, two adult rat skeletons and several juvenile ones were recovered from the bottom. They had made a bad choice for a nesting site. Most workmen took with them their day's supply of cider and a story is told in Broomfield of two carpenters who were building a new pulpit in the parish church when they were interrupted by the vicar. They were worried that he would disapprove of the cider in church and hid it behind their work. He talked for so long that they had finished the work, regretfully building the cider into the pulpit, before he went away.

Cider and cider vinegar feature in folk remedies for people and animals. Only recently a vet came across a case of cider being used to help stomach trouble in cattle. Cider has been thought good for rheumatism, although the reverse opinion is also heard. According to an old rhyme:

> Wold Zam could never goe vur long
> W'out his jar or virkin;
> A used the Zider zame'd twur ile
> To keep his joints vrim quirken.

One person calls regularly for cider vinegar to put in her bath to help rheumatism. It is also thought to be both a cure and cause of gout. An article in *The Lancet*, 21 September 1885, maintained that cider was good for the digestion since it is 'essentially diuretic', which is certainly the case with new cider juice. The article continued:

In Normandy, where the juice of the apple constitutes the staple drink of the lower classes, gout is said to be unknown save among the wealthy, who indulge in wine. Gravel and stone in the bladder are likewise very rare, and medical men are satisfied that the immunity from both these forms of disease should be placed to the credit of cider.

Sylas Taylor, in Evelyn's *Pomona*, extols its virtues, claiming that it 'does relax the belly ... aid concoction, depress Vapours, resist Melancholy, Spleen, Pleurisy, Strangury, and being sweetened with sugar abate inveterate Colds.'

Although claims for cider's medicinal qualities may be equivocal, many older people still drink a glass a day because they think it does them good. It is certainly appreciated as a cure for colds. One person remembered it being administered hot and spiced with ginger with toast, burnt black, floated in it. This potion had to be taken in bed because it would make the children incapable. Her father's mixture had whisky or brandy added, which he found a most pleasant cure.

Cider heated in copper, brass or tin utensils, was often found in local pubs. The 'cider shoe' was thrust into hot coals to warm the cider. To this was sometimes added ginger and gin, making a very warming beverage. Obliging bar-maids will still do this, but they heat it in a microwave oven!

In the fields, cider was generally drunk from a firkin, or poured into a horn beaker, but round the farm a pottery mug was used. These usually have two handles, but rarer ones have three. A correspondent wrote to the *Somerset Observer* on the subject of mugs in 1924. 'And what Somerset farmer would drink cider out of a cup with one handle! How could he hand it round to those seated with him in the chimney corner?' The mugs ranged in capacity from half a pint to half a gallon although the larger ones were kept for ceremonial occasions. Whole sets were made, graded in size. The pottery was usually fairly coarse but brightly patterned. Some pieces show hunting scenes or places or commemorate coronations or other events. The 'Farmer's Prayer' is often inscribed on one side:

Let the Wealthy and Great
Roll in Splendour and State
I envy them not I declare it.
I eat my own lamb
My own chickens and ham
I shear my own fleece and I wear it.
I have lawns, I have bowrs,
I have Fruit, I have flowrs,
The Lark is my morning alarmer,
So jolly boys now,
Here's God Speed the Plough,
Long Life and success to the Farmer.

Warming cider at the Hare and Hounds, Compton Dundon, at Christmas time during the 1930s.

Chapter 8
Somerset Orchards Today

While the chaffinch sings on the orchard bough
In England – now!
  Home Thoughts from Abroad, Robert Browning

It is perhaps symbolic that in the orchard of the Butcher's Arms at Carhampton where the annual wassailing traditionally takes place there is only one old apple tree left. And there are just one or two orchards left in a village where cider was once made at every farm and where even today, tradition and custom are celebrated in style.

Orchards are one of the most distinctive features of the traditional Somerset countryside, helping to create a small-scale, enclosed seasonal landscape where the pink and white blossoms of spring are followed by the deep rich green of foliage in summer and turning to a range of greens, reds and yellows in autumn as the fruit matures and ripens.

Many old orchards have occupied the same ground for hundreds of years and have undergone minimal regular regimes of grazing and cutting hay. They represent one of the last parts of the farm where the tractor does not disturb the soil by ploughing and have benefited from having few, if any, artificial inputs such as pesticides, herbicides and fertilisers, so consequently are ideal places for wild flowers, such as cowslips, primroses, hay rattle and ragged robin and even the common spotted and early purple orchids. Old orchards are valuable habitats for hares, and various species of wild bees and other insects. Owls, woodpeckers and jackdaws nest in the old tree trunks, blackbirds and bluetits shelter in the high hedges which often surround orchards, and in winter the last of the fruit on the ground is eaten eagerly by flocks of redwings and starlings. Red Admirals, commas and tortoiseshells love the juice of ripe fruit and may on occasion appear quite incapacitated by their enjoyment of it. Fruit plays an important part in the diet of hedgehogs, foxes and badgers while the old apple trees themselves are good hosts to lichens and mistletoe.

But in spite of a growing recognition of the importance of orchards in the landscape and as wildlife habitats, the traditional orchard is still being lost. Many of the old trees are becoming unstable and vulnerable to the winter gales. The decline in cidermaking in the period after the war has meant that new trees were not planted over several decades so that there are few coming to maturity. The location of many orchards on the edge of villages makes them attractive potential sites for housing development.

The diminution in the number of Somerset orchards which accompanied the decline in local cidermaking has been hastened in the last few years by government grants for grubbing up apple orchards in order to

Spraying in a commercial orchard.   James Ravilious

reduce the current over-production of culinary and dessert apples within the European Community. A series of substantial Apple Orchard Grubbing Up Grant Schemes in the 1990s encouraged producers to grub up young, healthy, well-stocked orchards in return for payments in 1996 of £4600 a hectare. It seems ironic that at the same time most of the juice for our established apple juice market is imported into this country in the form of concentrate.

Not every landowner has been tempted to grub up orchards and some have recognised that orchards can provide a reasonable income as well as a pleasant environment in which to work. The popularity of cider has increased enormously during the last decade and although the bulk of high alcohol ciders are produced from imported apple concentrate there is still a considerable demand for the more traditional product at the farm gate. The County Council has compiled a list of Somerset cider producers who are known to buy cider apples.

To stimulate interest in traditional orchards and encourage landowners to plant trees and replace those that are being lost, Somerset County Council in the 1990s grant-aided the planting of standard apple trees. The scheme, which involves a grant of about £10 a tree (approximately 40% of the cost), was met with considerable enthusiasm and hundreds of landowners have carried out schemes ranging from five trees to one hundred. From 1986 to 1996 grants encouraged the planting of some 15,000 standard trees and the level of interest increased tremendously. Many old orchards which might have been cleared away have been replanted and new ones established.

In 1992 the Countryside Commission included the management of traditional orchards as an eligible feature in the Countryside Stewardship scheme. This pilot project, designed to better integrate environmental and agricultural practices, involved ten-year agreements with landowners to manage orchards in return for government grants. The Farm and Rural Conservation Agency (FRCA) took over the scheme in 1997 and the number of orchards in management agreements is gradually increasing. While the stewardship scheme enables only a very small proportion of our traditional orchards to be protected, it represents the first move by central government to recognise their importance for landscape and nature conservation as well as for economic and cultural reasons. It is hoped that this support will grow in the future, reflecting the considerable public interest and concern which has become apparent in recent years.

Many people have become very enthusiastic about growing traditional Somerset varieties of apple both in private and commercial orchards. There are more than 150 to choose from (see Appendix 1), providing the opportunity not only to 'collect' them but to help conserve the varieties that not long ago were very rare or endangered. The nursery trade has also been encouraged to grow more standard trees as well as local apple varieties such as Lambrook Pippin, Stoke Red, Stembridge Jersey and Yarlington Mill. This not only helps to retain links with the past but also contributes to the identity and distinctiveness of Somerset orchards and apples.

Both existing and new orchards need to be managed properly and the County Council is encouraging this by listing a network of people who can give advice on matters such as tree-pruning, orchard management and cidermaking. The Farming Wildlife Advisory Group (FWAG) in Somerset, a trust run by farmers and landowners, recognised the need for more advice about orchard management and organise training days covering pruning, grafting and tree-planting.

The importance of managing orchards for high yields of fruit while at the same time demonstrating concern for the environment and encouraging growth of native flora, fauna and wildlife, was recognised in 1997 by the setting up by Matthew Clark plc, then Somerset's largest cidermaker, of the Green Apple award. This award was instigated for farmers and growers con-

Local children dance in Old Cleeve community orchard. John Atkins

tracted to produce apples for the company's two mills in Shepton Mallet and Taunton, in order to encourage them in sound environmental management techniques. The winning orchards demonstrated practices such as restricted use of herbicides and nitrogen fertilisers, hedge-laying to improve shelter for small birds and mammals, and leaving areas of grass and wild flowers unmown to attract beneficial insects and butterflies.

Awareness of the importance of orchards has been raised to a significant extent not only amongst landowners and farmers but the general public as well. This is largely due to the work of Common Ground, a national organisation which promotes recognition of our common cultural heritage, popular history and local places through links with the arts and the encouragement of local conservation projects, which began its Save our Orchards campaign in 1990.

Old friends reminisce while a youngster tries his hand at a nature quiz. The opening of Carhampton Community Orchard, 20 June 1998. David Nunn

Practical ideas put forward by Common Ground to help ordinary people care for old orchards and fruit trees included the setting up of community orchards. These offer a range of novel ideas for conserving traditional orchards or planting new ones. There are a number in Somerset and no two are alike but each provides a place, to a greater or lesser degree, for quiet contemplation, education and local festivities, a reservoir of local varieties and a refuge for wildlife.

Community orchards include those at Old Cleeve and Carhampton, both on land saved from being built over and now leased from the Crown Commisioners to provide havens of peace at the heart of the villages. New trees in traditional varieties are being planted to fill gaps caused by age and storm while hedges bearing fruit and nuts may soon replace untidy barbed-wire fences. A village orchard has been planted at Allerford while new orchards have been established at Barrington and Montacute by the National Trust and another at Norton-sub-Hamdon by the Woodland Trust. All help to restore the traditional village landscape of houses mixed in with gardens and fruit trees.

Common Ground recently introduced a new activity into our communities which is rapidly turning into a modern calendar custom, the celebration of Apple Day on 21 October or a nearby Saturday each year. Towns, villages, orchards and other organisations provide a programme of apple-based events to attract all ages. These range from the identification of apple varieties, competitions for apple cakes and chutney and demonstrations of pruning techniques to storytelling on an apple theme, the creation of apple hangings and sculptures and fun and games such as apple-bobbing, community renderings of apple and cider songs and traditional dancing.

Today many people are passionate about apples and orchards and it is their enthusiasm that may prove the saving grace for a precious and vulnerable aspect of Somerset's traditional landscape and way of life. Local collections of apple trees are making a vital contribution to the conservation of old and at-risk apple varieties throughout the United Kingdom. The continuation of familiar ways of making farmhouse cider as well as the steady growth of small-scale but commercial concerns still contribute to the maintenance of our well-loved orchards. A country way of life where cider was a regular and necessary part may have disappeared but the related landscapes, wildlife, scents of the countryside and sense of friendship and community are still ours for the asking as long as we continue to recognise the need to care for our orchards and not take them for granted.

A frog mug originally used at the Globe Inn, Walton.

ACKNOWLEDGEMENTS

FIRST EDITION

The research that originally led to the writing of this book was made possible by grant aid to the Somerset Rural Life Museum from Showerings Ltd of Shepton Mallet. The museum's thanks and mine go to them for their support and encouragement.

I should like to thank the following institutions and their staff for the help they have given during the cider research: Bath University Library; Blaise Castle House Museum, Bristol, Bridgwater Library; Harvey's Wine Museum, Bristol; Long Ashton Research Station, University of Bristol; Ministry of Agriculture, Fisheries and Food; Museum of Cider, Hereford; Museum of English Rural Life, Reading; National Farmers' Union; The Royal Bath and West and Southern Counties Society; Somerset College of Agriculture and Horticulture, Cannington; Somerset Rural Life Museum; Street Library; Woodspring Museum, Weston-super-Mare.

Special thanks to the following people: Anthea D'Aeth, Martyn Brown, John Dallimore, Les Davies, Ann Heeley.

The research was made possible by the participation of cidermakers and other local people throughout Somerset, and I should particularly like to thank the following: Mr R.N. Coate, Mr M. & Mr N. Dunkerton, Mr W.L. Dunkerton, Mr & Mrs K. Johnson, Mrs R.W. Mead, Mr H. Meade, Mr H. & Mr F. Naish, Mr C.A. Rose and Mr J. Whitehead.

Philippa Legg

SECOND EDITION

Thanks to Steve Scrivens and Phil Stone from the Environment Department, County Hall for encouragement, information and support in preparing this new edition; to Dr Robert Dunning, Mary Siraut and Janet Tall for additional information; to David Walker of Somerset Rural Life Museum and Liz Taynton of the Beaford Archive, Geoff Roberts and Mrs Perry for help with photographs.

Hilary Binding

ACKNOWLEDGEMENTS FOR ILLUSTRATIONS

The Beaford Centre holds James Ravilious's photographic archives;
Victor Bonham-Carter p.42; Harveys Wine Museum, Bristol p.7; Long Ashton Research Station for prints from Worlidge's *Treatise on Cider* and p.9; Chris Pearsall p.54; Peasedown St John Primary School p.23, p.46; Perry's of Dowlish Wake, cover and colour pictures 6 and 9; Somerset Record Office p.24; Times Newspapers Ltd p.17, p.22; Nancy Wells made the line drawings. The remaining photographs are held by the Rural Life Museum, Glastonbury.

Appendix 1: Apple Varieties of Somerset

Taken from *A Guide to the Origins of Somerset's Apples* by June Small

Date	Name	Origin	Type
1947	Ashton Bitter	Long Ashton	bittersweet cider
Early 20C	Ashton Brown Jersey	Long Ashton	bittersweet cider
Pre 1920	Blackwell Red	Backwell	cider
1872	Bailbrook Seedling	Bath	dessert
1893	Bartlett's Glory	Wells	dessert
1831	Bath Russet	Bath	
1864	Beauty of Bath	Bath	dessert
1883	Beauty of Wells	Wells	dessert
	Bell Apple/Sheep's Nose (Sweet Sheep's Nose)	Somerset/Devon border	cider, culinary
1872	Black Apple of Somerset		dessert
	Black Dabinett		med. sweet cider
	Black Valli		bittersweet cider
1665	Bridgwater Pippin	Bridgwater	culinary
	Broadleaf Jersey		cider
1884	Brockhead		dessert
1884	Brownsey		dessert, culinary?
1980s	Burrow Hill Early	Kingsbury Episcopi	full bittersweet cider
1934	Camelot		culinary, cider
Before 1920s	Cap of Liberty	Martock	bittersharp cider
1916	Cheddar Cross	Long Ashton	dessert
1934	Cheddar Pearmain	Long Ashton?	dessert
1883	Chelston Pie Maker	Wellington?	culinary
1950s	Chisel Jersey	Martock	full bittersweet cider
	Cider Lady's Finger		med. sharp cider
1950	Clarinette		culinary
1913	Clevedon Prolific		
	Coat Jersey	Coat, near Martock	bittersweet cider
1934	Coker Seedling	South Somerset?	culinary
1820-1830, 1884	College Apple		culinary
	Court Royal (Improved Pound)	Somerset/Devon border	sweet cider
1883	Covent Nonpareil		
1883	Cooper's Favourite	Bristol	
1883	Copman Thorpe Russet		
Pre-1790	Court De Wyck	Yatton	juicy rich flavour dessert
1895	Crimson King	Somerset/Devon border	culinary cider
1883	Curry Codlin	Curry Rivel, North Curry?	culinary
1961	Dabinett	Martock	bittersweet cider
1883	Darlington		dessert
1883	Dorchester		

Date	Name	Origin	Type
1934	Dorset	Long Ashton	
1957	Dove	Cadbury area	bittersweet cider
1940s	Dunkerton Late (sweet?)	Baltonsborough	bittersweet cider
1883	Dunnings Russet	Taunton	
1955	Early Blenheim		culinary, dessert
(1831) 1872	Early Pomeroy		dessert
1883	Even Permain	Taunton	
1924	Exeter Cross	raised Long Ashton	dessert
1831	Fair Maid of Taunton	Taunton	sharp dessert cider
1883	Fall Wine		acid cider
1957	Fill Barrell	Wincanton	bittersweet cider
1883	Fords Pippin	Bristol	
1934	Garland Long Keeper		dessert
1920s	Gatcombe	Long Ashton	sharp cider
1816	Glory of the West	Bridgwater	dessert, culinary
1913	Gloucester Cross	raised Long Ashton	dessert, culinary
1883	Golden Farmer	Merriott	dessert
1700s	Golden Knob	Bridgwater	sweet nutty dessert
1831	Gooseberry Apple		culinary
1934	Greasy Pippin	Somerset/Devon border	sharp cider
1883	Green Gribble		dessert
1883	Green Pearmain	Taunton	culinary
1883	Hagloe Pippin	Merriott	dessert
1883	Haigh Pippin		
1964	Hangdown (Horners)	probably Glastonbury	bittersweet cider
1910	Harry Masters Jersey	Yarlington	bittersweet cidere
1913	Hereford Cross	Long Ashton	dessert
1872	Hermans Pippin (1)		dessert
1883	Hermans Pippin (2)		culinary
1819	Hoary Morning		dessert, culinary
1883	Holberts Prince Albert		
1883	Hook St Pippin	Bristol	
1883	Husseys Pearmain		culinary
1800s	Kingston Black	Taunton	bittersharp cider
	Improved Dove	Stembridge	bittersweet cider
1934	Lambrook Pippin	Lambrook	cider
1934	Lambrook Seedling	Lambrook	dessert
	Langworthy	Somerset/Devon border	sharp cider
1883	Liddons Prolific		culinary
1872	Lord Suffolk		dessert cider?
1883	Madeline		dessert
1928	Maggie Greive	raised Long Ashton	dessert
1920s	Major		full bittersweet cider
1883	Mealy Late Blossom	Taunton	culinary

Date	Name	Origin	Type
1948	Melmoth	Yeovil	dessert
1872	Merchant Apple	Ilminster	culinary, dessert
187	Morgan Sweet		dessert, cider
1884	Knotted Kernel		
1883	Morning Thorpe Pippin (1)		
1883	Morning Thorpe Pippin (2)		
1946	Muriel	Yeovil	
1934	Nailsea White	North Somerset	culinary
1894	Nelds Dropper	Long Ashton	
1920	Nelsons Glory	Bristol	culinary
1920	Newport Cross	Long Ashton	
1824	Nine Square	Somerton	sweet dessert
1800s	Old Somerset Russet		dessert
1872	Parkers Glory Pippin	Merriott?	sweet dessert
1883	Pawn Apple		dessert
	Pennard Bitter	Pennard	bittersweet cider
1916	Plymouth Cross	raised Long Ashton	culinary
1851	Pomeroy of Somerset	Taunton?	dessert
1824	Poormans Profit		dessert?
1962	Porters Perfection	East Lambrook	bittersharp cider
1888	Pound Apple		dessert
1700s	Powells Russet		dessert
1883	Puffin		dessert
1934	Pyleigh	Long Ashton	
1842	Queen Anne		
1934	Radcliffe Nonpareil	Long Ashton	dessert
	Red Jersey		cider
	Red Worthy	Martock	cider
1903	Rich's Favourite	Churchill	
1880	Rough Pippin		dessert
1883	Royal George	Taunton	culinary
	Royal Jersey (1)		
	Royal Jersey (2)		
1818	Royal Somerset	Somerset/Devon border	sharp cider, culinary
1818	Sack & Sugar	Somerset/Devon border	dessert
1919	St Ivel Pippin	Yeovil	
1950	Sandew		cider? culinary
1883	Sheep's Nose (1)		mild ciders
1872	Sheep's Nose (2)		culinary
1884	Shoreditch White	Taunton?	culinary
	Silver Cup		cider
1883	Slack me Girdle	South Somerset	sweet cider
1883	Small Catshead	Taunton	culinary
1831	Somerset Lasting	Devon/Somerset border	culinary

Date	Name	Origin	Type
1800s	Somerset Redstreak		bittersweet cider
1905	Sops in Wine	Devon/Somerset border	culinary, cider
	Stable Jersey	Shepton Mallet	cider
	Stembridge Cluster	Stembridge	med. bittersweet cider
	Stembridge Jersey	Stembridg	cider
1800s	Stoke Red (Never Blight)		bittersharp cider
1950	Stoke Allow		med. bittersweet cider
1934	Squires Codlin	Merriott?	dessert
1831	Summer Stibber		dessert
1883	Sweet Achan	Merriott	dessert
	Sweet Blenheim (Court Royal)		cider
1919	Taunton Cross	raised Long Ashton Taunton	dessert
1851	Taunton Golden Pippin	Taunton	dessert
1872	Taunton Nonpareil	Taunton	
	Taylors Sweet	North Cadbury	sweet cider
1883	Thomage Seedling	Merriott	
1700s	Tom Putt	Trent	culinary, sharp cider
	Tremletts Bitter	Exe Vale?	bittersweet cider
1967	Underleaf	Long Ashton	
1883	Waterloo Pippin		
1930	White Close Pippin	North Cadbury	bittersweet cider
1883	White Jersey		bittersweet cider
1883	Whittles Dumpling	Taunton	culinary
1883	Wildings Redstreak	Merriott	cider? culinary
1899	Winter Hilary		
	Woodbine (several varieties)		
1920	Worcester Cros	raised Long Ashton	
1900s	Yarlington Mill	Yarlington	bittersweet cider
	Yeovil Sour	Yeovil	

Appendix 2: Somerset Rural Life Museum

Cider Orchard

TRADITIONAL SOMERSET CIDER APPLE VARIETIES

Tremlett's Bitter
Dunkerton Sweet
Kingston Black
Yarlington Mill
Stoke Red
Chisel Jersey
Stembridge Jersey
Morgan Sweet

TRADITIONAL CIDER APPLE VARIETY (GLOUCESTERSHIRE)

Genette Moyle

SOMERSET CIDER/DESSERT APPLE

Tom Putt

NEWER CIDER APPLE VARIETIES

Browns Apple
Michelin
Muscadet

NEWER CULINARY APPLE VARIETY

Bramley Seedling

Bibliography

Acland. I. H. & Sturge. W., *The farming of Somersetshire* (1851).

Aubrey, I., *Remains of gentilisme* (1686).

Beale, J., *Herefordshire orchards: a pattern for all England* (1657).

Billingsley, J., *General view of the agriculture of the county of Somerset* (1797).

Bowyer, P. B., *A history of cidermaking in England* (Brighton Polytechnic unpublished thesis, 1977).

Cooke, C. W. K., 'A lecture ... on cider', *Journal of the Society of Arts* (8 March 1895).

Evelyn, J., *Kalendarium hortense* (1664).

Fothergill, A., 'Experiments and observations on cyder-wine', *Bath and West of England Society Letters and Papers* 5 (1790).

Grenville, K. N., *Some practical hints on cider-making, Royal Agricultural Society of England Journal.* 62 (1901).

Hogg, K. & Bull, H. G., *The Herefordshire pomona* (1876-85).

Knight, T. A., *Pomona Herefordiensis* (1811).

Knight, T. A, *A treatise on the culture of the apple and pear, and on the manufacture of cider and perry* (1797).

Marshall, W., *Rural economy of the West of England* (1796).

Minchinton, W. E., 'The British cider industry since 1870', *National Westminster Bank Quarterly Review* (November 1975).

Minchinton, W. E., 'Cider and folklore', *Folk Life.* 13 (1975).

Parsons, J. W., *On cider, Bath and West of England Society Letters and Papers* 12 (1810).

Philips, J., *Cyder: a poem* (1708).

Pidgeon, D., 'The trials of cidermaking plant at Glastonbury', *Royal Agricultural Society of England Journal*, 3rd Series. 1 (1890).

Pollard, A. & Beech, F. W., *Cider making* (1957).

Read, J., *Cluster-O'-Vive* (1923).

Somerset County Herald newspaper cuttings in the Somerset Studies Library, Taunton (ca 1920-60).

Victoria History of Somerset. vol. 2 (1911).

Wallace, I. & Marsh, J. W., *Science and fruit* (1953).

Watson, W. G. W., *Somerset life and character* (1924).

Worlidge, J., *Vinetum Britannicum; or a treatise of cider* (1676).

For those wishing to explore the subject further, the material collected during the cider research project which led to this publication has been deposited in the Somerset Rural Life Museum, Abbey Farm, Bere Lane, Glastonbury.